Journal of Beckett Studies

Volume 19 Number 2 2010

T0371006

Edinburgh University Press

Subscription Rates for Volume 20

		UK	Rest of World	N. America
Institutions	Print	£79.00	£83.00	£150.00
	Online	£71.00	£71.00	£128.00
	Print and online	£99.00	£104.00	£188.00
	Back issues/ single copies	£41.00	£45.00	£83.00
Individuals	Print	£33.00	£37.00	$64.00
	Online	£33.00	£33.00	£58.00
	Print and online	£41.00	£46.00	$80.00
	Back issues/ single copies	£17.00	£19.00	£35.00

Postage

Print only and print plus online prices include packaging and airmail for subscribers in North America. Print only and print plus online subscriptions for subscribers in the Rest of the world include packaging and surface mail postage. Please add a further £6 if you would like your subscription posted by airmail.

Payment options

All orders must be accompanied by the correct payment. You can pay by cheque in Pound Sterling or US Dollars, bank transfer, Direct Debit or Credit/Debit Card. The individual rate applies only when a subscription is paid for with a personal cheque, credit card or bank transfer from a personal account.

To order using the online subscription form, please visit www.eupjournals.com/jobs/page/subscribe

To place your order by credit card, phone +44 (0)131 650 6207, fax on +44 (0)131 662 3286 or email journals@eup.ed.ac.uk. Don't forget to include the expiry date of your card, the security number (three digits on the reverse of the card) and the address that the card is registered to.

Cheques must be made payable to Edinburgh University Press Ltd. Sterling cheques must be drawn on a UK bank account.

If you would like to pay by bank transfer or Direct Debit, contact us at journals@eup.ed.ac.uk and we will provide instructions.

Advertising

Advertisements are welcomed and rates are available on request, or by consulting our website at www.eupjournals.com. Advertisers should send their enquiries to the Journals Marketing Manager at the address above.

Transferred to Digital Print 2011
Printed and bound by CPI Group (UK) Ltd, Croydon, CR0 4YY

JOURNAL OF BECKETT STUDIES
VOLUME 19 NUMBER 2 2010

MARK NIXON AND DIRK VAN HULLE

Introduction

The importance of Germany to Beckett's work no longer needs to be established. The depth and range of his engagement with German culture was firmly outlined by James Knowlson's 1996 *Damned to Fame*, and by critical studies before and after the publication of that landmark biography. Indeed, when the Barbican in London staged a roundtable discussion of 'Beckett's Nations' in 2006, Germany joined Ireland and France in a triumvirate of cultural determinants of influence. Beckett's knowledge of German literature, music, art and philosophy has received extensive treatment, especially in terms of specific proponents from that tradition: Schubert, Schopenhauer, Mauthner, Kant, Goethe and Hölderlin to mention only the most obvious. Beckett's relationship with the German language, as well as his work in German theatres and television studios following on from his directorial debut with *Godot* at the Schiller Theater in Berlin in 1965, have also been the object of scholarly scrutiny. At the same time, Beckett's influence on post-war German cultural and socio-political discourses has been profound, as is attested by several studies.[1] In these evaluations of the importance of Germany to Beckett, archival resources have played a central role. This is especially the case with the 'German

Journal of Beckett Studies 19.2 (2010): 151–153
Edinburgh University Press
DOI: 10.3366/E0309520710000567
© The editors, *Journal of Beckett Studies*
www.eupjournals.com/jobs

Diaries', six notebooks kept by Beckett during his trip through Germany from October 1936 to April 1937, which have been the focus of many critical studies as well as exhibitions. Beyond these diaries, there are other important documents: Beckett's German language and vocabulary notebooks, notes on German literary history, extensive extracts from Goethe's work and of course the theatrical notebooks, testifying to Beckett's directorial work in Germany.

This is the first issue of the *Journal of Beckett Studies* to concentrate on Beckett and Germany, and can be aligned with similar volumes on Ireland (Vol. 2, No. 2, Spring 1993) and France (Vol. 4, No. 1, Autumn 1994). The first part of the volume will be of particular interest to Beckett scholars, as it presents, for the first time in English translation, Theodor W. Adorno's unpublished notes on Beckett. They were compiled, introduced and annotated by Rolf Tiedemann in the *Frankfurter Adorno Blätter* (published by the Theodor W. Adorno Archiv in 1994). Tiedemann's documentation contains Adorno's notes on meetings with Beckett, on *Endgame* and on *The Unnamable*, as well as the marginalia in his copy of Elmar Tophoven's German translation *Der Namenlose*. The notes on *Endgame* resulted in the publication of Adorno's influential essay 'Trying to Understand *Endgame*' ('Versuch, das Endspiel zu verstehen'). His notes on *The Unnamable* were also kept with a view towards a more extensive treatment, but this project was left unfinished at the time of the German thinker's death in 1969. The present Adorno dossier focuses on his notes on *Endgame* and *The Unnamable*, translated by Dirk Van Hulle and Shane Weller with accompanying essays that situate the notes within the context of Adorno's work and assess the affinity between Adorno and Beckett.

Gaby Hartel, in her essay, examines Beckett in the context of early radio theories, remarking in particular the importance of Rudolf Arnheim's work when thinking about Beckett's own radio pieces. The following essay, by Tine Koch, investigates Beckett's dialogue with Schlegel's work from both a literary and a philosophical perspective, and extends our understanding of Beckett's relationship with German romanticism.

As a reader of German literature and as an aspiring art critic, Beckett went to Germany at an extremely tumultuous and dangerous period in the country's political and cultural history. First published in German in 2005, Mark Nixon's chronology of this journey through Germany in 1936/37, based on the 'German Diaries', gives a valuable summary of these unpublished documents.

The review section, we think, forms a central part of the issue. It is regrettable that Beckett Studies in Germany, which is thriving, is not more widely known beyond its borders, and these reviews aim to alert scholars of the important work that has been done since 2005. Finally, as with other issues of *JOBS*, further production and book reviews, not connected directly with Germany, are included at the end.

It is the editors' hope that this issue of the journal will add to current scholarship surrounding the topic 'Beckett and Germany', and will also help to establish a more substantial dialogue between scholars working in different cultural and linguistic contexts. As a polyglot writer, Beckett would surely have approved.

On a final, sad, note, we wish to acknowledge the recent passing of three people who were important to Beckett and collaborated with him on important works: the critic and translator Barbara Bray, the actor Pierre Chabert, and the visual artist Avigdor Arikha. Their contribution to the field will be acknowledged more fully in a future issue of the *Journal of Beckett Studies*.

NOTE

1. See for example the three essays on Beckett's reception in Germany (East and West) in *The International Reception of Samuel Beckett* (2009), ed. Mark Nixon and Matthew Feldman, London: Continuum.

Dossier: Adorno's Notes on Beckett

THEODOR W. ADORNO

Notes on Beckett[*]

Translated by Dirk Van Hulle and Shane Weller

In 1994, the *Frankfurter Adorno Blätter* (published by the Theodor W. Adorno Archiv) published a dossier, compiled, introduced and annotated by Rolf Tiedemann, documenting Adorno's reading of Beckett's works. Tiedemann notes that Adorno worked on his essay 'Versuch, das Endspiel zu verstehen' from the summer of 1960 to the next spring (Tiedemann, 1994, 26). The text of the essay was mainly written in September 1961. At the end of that month, on 27 February 1961, he presented parts of it at the celebration in Beckett's honour, organised by the German publisher Suhrkamp in Frankfurt am Main.

The next year, in the spring of 1962, Adorno read *L'Innommable* in a first edition of the German translation by Elmar Tophoven (1959), making notes, both in the margins and on seven pages of the preliminary pages of his copy of *Der Namenlose*. Rolf Tiedemann also provides some notes Adorno took after a few conversations

[*] Adorno's notes on Beckett were first published in *Frankfurter Adorno Blätter III* (1994). They appear here in English with the permission of Suhrkamp Verlag, Berlin.

Journal of Beckett Studies 19.2 (2010): 157–178
Edinburgh University Press
DOI: 10.3366/E0309520710000579
www.eupjournals.com/jobs

with Samuel Beckett (between 1958 and 1968) and a letter Adorno
sent to Beckett on 4 February 1969.

The present translation focuses on the notes Adorno took to
prepare his essay 'Versuch, das Endspiel zu verstehen' (relating the
notes to relevant corresponding passages in the essay, translated as
'Trying to Understand *Endgame*' by Michael T. Jones, *New German
Critique* 26, Spring-Summer 1982, pp. 119–50, and by Shierry Weber
Nicholsen in Theodor W. Adorno, *Notes to Literature*, New York:
Columbia University Press, 1991, pp. 241–75) and on his notes for
a planned, but never realised essay on *L'Innommable*. Whenever
Adorno had used a particular note while he was writing up his
essay on *Endgame*, he usually struck it through. To indicate this, we
have applied Rolf Tiedemann's editorial notation, marking these
passages by striking through their source reference. An indication
of corresponding passages in Michael T. Jones's translation of
the essay follows after the relevant note; page references to the
German original in *Noten zur Literatur* (Adorno, 1981) are followed
by the page numbers in Jones's translation (Adorno, 1982). The
aim in this translation has been to preserve the telegraphic
and sometimes awkward phrasing of the German. On occasion,
however, words or phrases have been added for clarification: these
appear in square brackets. All underlinings are in the original.
The translation follows the chronology of Adorno's notes; the two
essays discussing these notes follow the chronology of Beckett's
works. We wish to thank Mark Nixon, Ben Hutchinson and Anna
Katharina Schaffner for their extremely helpful suggestions on the
translation.

Translation of Adorno's Notes on *Endgame*

[note 1] One of the possible aspects: literature in the age of the
impossibility of humour. What has become of humour. Residual
humour. – Humour as regression (clown).
    (~~Notebook G, p. 83~~)

[300; trans. 134: 'Psychoanalysis explains clownish humor as a
regression back to a primordial ontogenetic level, and Beckett's

regressive play descends to that level. But the laughter it inspires ought to suffocate the laughter. That is what happened to humor, after it became – as an aesthetic medium – obsolete (…)']

[note 2] In empirical existence there are innumerable situations which – detached from their pragmatic and psychological context – *objectively* assume an expression of their own. An old man takes a nap and pulls a handkerchief over his eyes. Completely harmless in natural life: the horror that emanates from it when isolated in a tableau vivant. B[eckett]'s method consists in releasing such situations and their expression, assembling them in a second, autonomous context. Affinity with the relationship between music and intentions. In a desultory way already in Kafka; in B[eckett] turned into a consistent principle (like serial music vis-à-vis Schönberg). NB Beckett's criticism of Kafka.
    (~~Notebook G, p. 87ff.~~)

[297–98; trans. 132: 'then "HAMM: Old stancher! (*Pause.*) You… remain." Such situations, emancipated from their context and from personal character, are reconstructed in a second autonomous context, just as music joins together the intentions and states of expression immersed in it until its sequence becomes a structure in its own right.']

[note 3] The background. In *The Wild Duck*, Hjalmar forgets to bring the menu of the dinner at the old Werle's to his daughter, as promised. This is psychologically motivated and at the same time symbolic in the strict sense of Freudian parapraxis. When this symbolism is disconnected from its psychological determination, it simultaneously acquires an objective, concrete aspect; it becomes the carrier of the dramatic idea, as in the later works (e.g. the clerk [Vilhelm Foldal] being run over in *John Gabriel Borkman*). If, from these objective symbols, one extracts those meanings, the relationship with the – problematic – idea, one is left with code signs of an x. That is the genesis of the absurd. – Beckett relates to Kafka the way the serial composers relate to Schönberg. His

criticism of Kafka contains the same problem as the integral composition in its relationship to the antagonistic one.

(~~Notebook G, p. 93~~)

[304; trans. 137: 'What becomes of form in *Endgame* can be virtually reconstructed from literary history. In Ibsen's *The Wild Duck*, the degenerate photographer Hjalmar Ekdal – himself a potential anti-hero (...) the accountant Foldal is overcome by so-called "youth."']

[305; trans. 137: 'Drama need only become aware of the ineluctably ridiculous nature of such pan-symbolism, which destroys itself; it need only take that up and utilise it, and Beckettian absurdity is already achieved as a result of the immanent dialectic of form. Not meaning anything becomes the only meaning.']

[303; trans. 136: 'Beckett's drama is heir to Kafka's novels, to whom he stands in a similar relation as the serial composers to Schönberg.']

[note 4] The great closing scene in *Fin de partie* is the parody of the *scène à faire*, become impossible.

(Notebook G, p. 97)

[note 5] The origin of the notion of the situation in Jaspers has to be noted, and at the same time the difference from it – from his subjectivism – needs to be sharply determined. In this regard, compare Rickert's passage on the physiognomy of the objective mind.

(Notebook G, p. 100.1)

[294; trans. 129: 'It [the "situation"] is defined by Jaspers as "a reality for an existing subject who has a stake in it" (...) he also calls it "not just a reality governed by natural laws. It is a sense-related reality," a reality moreover which, strangely enough, is said by Jaspers to be "neither psychological nor physical, but both in one." When situation becomes – in Beckett's view – actually both, it loses its existential-ontological constituents: personal identity and meaning.']

[295; trans. 130: 'These Beckettian situations which constitute his drama are the negative of meaningful reality. (...) Beckett's treatment of these situations, that panicky and yet artificial derivation of simplistic slapstick comedy of yesteryear, articulates a content noted already in Proust. In his posthumous work *Immediacy and Sense-Interpretation*, Heinrich Rickert considers the possibility of an objective physiognomy of mind (...)']

[note 6] The enigmatic and the physiognomy of the objective mind. The situations say something – but what? NB very similar to music. (Notebook G, p. 100.2)

[296; trans. 130–31: 'The physiognomy of objective expression however retains an enigma. The situations say something, but what?' (...) Proust, in a subterranean mystical tradition, still clings affirmatively to that physiognomy, as if involuntary memory disclosed a secret language of things; in Beckett, it becomes the physiognomy of what is no longer human. (...) [132] Such situations, emancipated from their context and from personal character, are reconstructed in a second autonomous context, just as music joins together the intentions and states of expression (...)']

[note 7] The simplest not to be withheld: the experience of existence as absurd. Yet this experience is not ontological but historical.* [*(note by Adorno) Absurdity has its historical side: for people do not themselves determine their lives in a transparent way.] The basis of this experience is the loss of faith in providence and a meaningful encapsulation of life; the explosion of cosmology; the dilapidation and problematisation of order-producing structures to which that meaning used to be attached; the immediate threat to the survival of the species. As soon as reason, released and terminal, needs to look for a meaning, it has no other answer than this nothingness: it is the apriori of the question. In this context, it is crucial that such historical answers always *necessarily appear* to be ontological, without history; that is precisely the blinding element, the bewitchment. B[eckett]'s genius is that he has captured this semblance of the non-historical, of the *condition humaine*, in historical images, and thus transfixed it. The ideology of the *condition humaine* is replaced by dialectical images. (Notebook G, p. 100ff.)

[287; trans. 123: 'What would be called the *condition humaine* in existentialist jargon is the image of the last human, which is devouring the earlier ones—humanity. Existential ontology asserts the universally valid in a process of abstraction which is not conscious of itself. While it still—according to the old phenomenological doctrine of the intuition of essence—behaves as if it were aware, even in the particular, of its binding determinations, thereby unifying apriority and concreteness, it nonetheless distills out what appears to transcend temporality.']

[319; trans. 148: 'The historical inevitability of this absurdity allows it to seem ontological; that is the veil of delusion produced by history itself. Beckett's drama rips through this veil. The immanent contradiction of the absurd, reason terminating in senselessness, emphatically reveals the possibility of a truth which can no longer even be thought; it undermines the absolute claim exercised by what merely is. Negative ontology is the negation of ontology: history alone has brought to maturity what was appropriated by the mythic power of timelessness.']

[note 8] There is something absurd in the form of the dialogue itself; meaninglessness of the question-and-answer relationship; gibberish (connection with Ionesco); chatter as trivial reflex of the objective world, second language. Hearing oneself talking is like watching a Beckett play. *Analyse this moment accurately.* One is alienated from one's own language by B[eckett].* [*(note by Adorno) Situation: One cannot talk any longer. Text p. 22.]
    (Notebook G, p. 102)

[305; trans. 138: 'Rather than striving to liquidate the discursive element of language through pure sound, Beckett turns that element into an instrument of its own absurdity and he does that according to the ritual of clowns, whose babbling becomes nonsensical by presenting itself as sense. The objective disintegration of language—that simultaneously stereotyped and faulty chatter of self-alienation, where word and sentence melt together in human mouths—penetrates the aesthetic arcanum. The second language of those falling silent, a conglomeration of insolent phrases, pseudo-logical connections, and galvanised words appearing as commodity signs – as the desolate echo of the advertising world – is "refunctioned" (*umfunktioniert*) into the language of a poetic work that negates language. Beckett thus approximates the drama of Eugène Ionesco.']

[note 9] The play is the only attempt in grand style to hold out against the potential of total destruction – like Picasso's *Guernica*, Schönberg's *Survivor* [*from Warsaw*, Op. 46, 1947] against the horrors of the Hitler era. With utmost decisiveness B[eckett] has stuck to the narrow ridge of what is still possible. On the one hand he has realised that absolute destruction – to which no individual human being's experience extends – cannot become thematic directly. The word atom does not appear (although it does in the corollary *All That Fall*). There are no atomic conflicts à la *Blaues Licht*. Everything is shown only through the reflection of the experience, as it were in a subcutaneous expressionistic inwardness (reminiscent of Strindberg's *Dödsdansen* [*The Dance of Death*]). Absolute limit of technological utopia, of science fiction. But at the same time the possibility of experience, and the number of subjects, is so reduced that it can only be conceived as a consequence of the catastrophe. In a way the latter endorses the process of historical regression. – On the other hand nothing evaporates into the purely symbolical. The situations are real, and they are pragmatic presuppositions (partial end of the world), developed with utmost discretion. Parody of the exposition in traditional drama, in which the background information is presented, dispersed (end of organic life, the sunken lighthouse. The protagonists' blindness and paralysis as consequence of the catastrophe?[)] – It is as if consciousness wished to endure the end of its own physical presence, while looking it in the face. Connection with Proust.

   (~~Notebook G, p. 103ff.~~)

[321; trans. 150: 'Consciousness begins to look its own demise in the eye, as if it wanted to survive the demise, as these two want to survive the destruction of their world. Proust, about whom the young Beckett wrote an essay, is said to have attempted to keep protocol on his own struggle with death, in notes which were to be integrated into the description of Bergotte's death. *Endgame* carries out this intention like a mandate from a testament.']

[note 10] In my work on Kafka, I have reproached Gide for his stage adaptation [of Kafka's *The Trial*], arguing that drama is not possible without subject and freedom. That is where *Fin de partie* sets in. The question is: what is possible in terms of drama without subject and without the possibility of freedom. It is precisely in this way that the play becomes a parody of drama and all its categories.
(Notebook G, p. 105)

[302; trans. 136: 'Dramatic categories as a whole are treated just like humor. All are parodied. But not ridiculed. (...)']

[note 11] Parody of drama = drama in the age of its impossibility. In tragedy, stychomythia served as a tool to tighten the dramatic tension to the utmost: quintessence of antithesis. Here it turns into slackening: less and less talkative protagonists, complete regression (as in positivism: talking in short sentences).
(Notebook G, p. 106.1)

[303; trans. 136–37: 'For example, tragedy, at the height of its plot and with antithesis as its quintessence [trans. Weber: 'as the quintessence of antithesis'; Adorno, 1991, 260], manifested the utmost tightening of the dramatic thread, stichomythia – dialogues in which the trimester spoken by one person follows that of the other. (...) Beckett employs it as if the detonation had revealed what was buried in drama. *Endgame* contains rapid, monosyllabic dialogues, like the earlier question-and-answer games between the blinded king and fate's messenger. But where the bind tightened then, the speakers now grow slack. Short of breath until they almost fall silent, they no longer manage the synthesis of linguistic phrases; they stammer in protocol sentences that might stem from positivists or Expressionists.']

[note 12] The Endgame is a draw, isn't it?
(Notebook G, p. 106.2)

[note 13] Tremendous richness of allusions and links: the malignant joke, she cries ergo she lives etc., as in [Herman] Bang.
  (Notebook G, p. 107)

[note 14] The relation to history is expressed by means of a *taboo*. The shock is such that it cannot be talked about. It is even noticeable in the way the play is composed. The catastrophe, which is clearly the pragmatic presupposition, cannot be named. Corresponds more or less to the way people in Germany in 1960 talk about the murder of the Jews in attenuating allusions.
  (Notebook G, p. 109ff.)

[287; trans. 123: 'The violence of the unspeakable is mimicked by the timidity to mention it. Beckett keeps it nebulous. One can only speak euphemistically about what is incommensurate with all experience, just as one speaks in Germany of the murder of the Jews.']

[note 15] What about the game of chess?

  1) the empty field, remainder, the destruction only allegorically readable in the result.
  2) endgames are regulated, prescribed by a system; they can only change by means of errors, not by means of preferences.
  3) as in chess, winners and losers are dependent on each other.
  4) chess as a *situation* (separated from human beings, and yet they are present through the agency of the king. The king is the remainder of the subject). The meaninglessness, the folly in the game's seriousness.
  5) in the endgame, the best that can happen to the losing party is a *draw*. Situations such as stalemate, perpetual check. Bad infinity.

(Notebook G, p. 110ff.)

[288; trans. 125: 'Drama falls silent and becomes gesture, frozen amid the dialogues. Only the result of history appears – as decline.']

[316; trans. 146: 'The field is almost empty, and what happened before can only be poorly construed from the positions of the few remaining figures.']

[316; trans. 146: 'Only artistic mistakes or accidents, such as something growing somewhere, could cause unforeseen events (...)']

[316; trans. 146: 'Hamm is the king, about whom everything turns and who can do nothing himself. The incongruity between chess as pastime and the excessive effort involved (...)']

[316; trans. 146: 'Whether the game ends with stalemate or with perpetual check, or whether Clov wins, remains unclear, as if clarity in that would already be too much meaning.']

[293; trans. 128: 'While meanings in Kafka were beheaded or confused, Beckett calls a halt to the bad infinity of intentions: their sense is senselessness.']

[note 16] *Beckett*[:] something about existentialism's change of function and its cause needs to be included in the text
    (~~Notebook G, p. 111~~)

[note 16a] 'simple fare' [*Hausmannskost*]: The totalitarians' ranting against decadence has its reason. It has to do with utopia. What a quantity of satiation, tedium, *dégoût* is needed to want something that would be completely different. The newcomer is impressed by everything that *is*, to such an extent that he never rises against it. Health means: to make do with the nourishment offered. (see Tiedemann, 1994, 75 note 28)

> [283–84; trans. 121: 'Totalitarians like Lukács, who rage against the – truly terrifying – simplifier as "decadent," are not ill advised by the interests of their bosses. They hate in Beckett what they have betrayed. Only the nausea of satiation – the tedium of spirit with itself – wants something completely different: prescribed "health" nevertheless makes do with the nourishment offered, with simple fare. Beckett's dégoût cannot be forced to fall in line.']

[note 17] A primitive historical intention would be just as senseless as the ontological intention attributed to B[eckett] by Lukács.

No struggle against atomic death. Neither *condition humaine* nor *Ape and Essence*. A third option: the horror of the whole flares up in – *only* in – that of the last element (proofs). The human being as what he became. The fate of the species is decided upon on its last day – as in utopia.

B[eckett]'s refusal to explain (difference from Sartre and Camus) corresponds with the unsolvability. But as little of a realist or realist-symbolist as Kafka. Whereas in Kafka meaning is broken off or confused, one could perhaps say that in B[eckett] the meaning is the meaninglessness (parody of philosophy, which transfigures thrownness into meaning). But it is not a universal – which would turn it into an idea again – but the expression of more specific situations than its horror.

(~~Notebook G, p. 112ff.~~)

[293; trans. 128: 'While meanings in Kafka were beheaded or confused, Beckett calls a halt to the bad infinity of intentions: their sense is senselessness. Objectively and without any polemical intent, that is his answer to existential philosophy, which under the name of "thrownness" and later of "absurdity" transforms senselessness itself into sense, exploiting the equivocations inherent in the concept of sense. To this Beckett juxtaposes no world view, rather he takes it at its word. What becomes of the absurd, after the characters of the meaning of existence have been torn down, is no longer a universal – the absurd would then be yet again an idea – but only pathetic details which ridicule conceptuality (...)']

[note 18] Heidegger's states of being [*Befindlichkeiten*], Jaspers' situations have become materialistic in B[eckett]. The threshold against existentialism is the denial of inwardness.

(Notebook G, p. 114.1)

[293; trans. 129: 'Removed from their inwardness, Heidegger's states of being (*Befindlichkeiten*) and Jaspers' "situations" have become materialistic (...) As soon as the subject is no longer doubtlessly self-identical, no longer a closed structure of meaning, the line of demarcation with the exterior becomes blurred, and the situations of inwardness become at the same time physical ones.']

[note 19] The humour of the last human being: that is the humour that can no longer count on any laughing. B[eckett] has recovered for humour what otherwise only applies to the categories of the Arts with a capital A – which he tacitly liquidates: the resignation of communication.
    (Notebook G, p. 114.2)

   [301; trans. 134: 'Beckett carries out the verdict on humor. The jokes of the damaged people are themselves damaged. They no longer reach anybody (...)']
   [307; trans. 139: 'Communication, the universal law of clichés, proclaims that there is no more communication. The absurdity of all speaking is not unrelated to realism but rather develops from it. For communicative language postulates – already in its syntactic form, through logic, the nature of conclusions, and stable concepts – the principle of sufficient reason. Yet this requirement is hardly met anymore (...)']

[note 20] The play takes place in a no man's land, a zone of indifference between inner and outer. What remains of these two in a state of complete alienation. Concentration camp, intermediate domain between life and death, life as a knacker's yard.
    (Notebook G, p. 114ff.)

   [292; trans. 127–28: '*Endgame* takes place in a zone of indifference between inner and outer, neutral between – on the one hand – the "materials" without which subjectivity could not manifest itself or even exist, and – on the other – an animating impulse which blurs the materials, as if that impulse had breathed on the glass through which they are viewed.']
   [293; trans. 128: '*Endgame* occupies the nadir of what philosophy's construction of the subject-object confiscated at its zenith: pure identity becomes the identity of annihilation, identity of subject and object in the state of complete alienation.']

[note 21] Essence and existentialism. Break from rationalism. Focus on the essential. Expression of increasing irrationality. Through polemic against rationalism and positivism *not* apologetic. Lacking the theological, both open and hidden. – Residues of global annihilation.
(Notebook G, p. 115.1)

[note 22] Existence in Beckett: minimum of existence.
(Notebook G, p. 115.2)

[284; trans. 121: 'Existentialism itself is parodied; nothing remains of its "invariants" other than minimal existence.']

[note 23] Compare with chapter 6 in my Kafka, beware of overlap.
(Notebook G, p. 115.3)

[Theodor W. Adorno (1998), 'Aufzeichnungen zu Kafka', in *Gesammelte Schriften* 10.1 (Kulturkritik und Gesellschaft I), Darmstadt: Wissenschaftliche Buchgesellschaft, pp. 271–73.]

[note 24] Parody of both philosophy and drama (the two converge: revolt against the content).
(Notebook G, p. 115.4)

[284; trans. 121: 'He responds to the cheery call to play along with parody, parody of the philosophy spit out by his dialogues as well as parody of forms.']

[note 25] The end of the world is already discounted.
(Notebook G, p. 115.5)

[286; trans. 123: 'The end of the world is discounted, as if it were a matter of course. Every supposed drama of the atomic age would mock itself, if only because its fable would hopelessly falsify the horror of historical anonymity by shoving it into the characters and actions of humans (...)']

[note 26] No individual can lodge complaint any longer (Wolfskehl). He [Beckett] does not indict society. Certainly not, and that is precisely the spearhead which he aims at it. Against Lukács

and vulgar Marxist interpretation. – Presupposition that all of that
is *smothered*. In time. In addition the missed moment.
  (Notebook G, p. 116)

[290, trans. 126: 'The vanity of the individual who indicts
society, while his rights themselves merge in the accumulation
of the injustice of all individuals – disaster itself – is manifest
in embarrassing declamations like the "Germany" poem of
Karl Wolfskehl. The "too-late," the missed moment condemns
such bombastic rhetoric to phraseology. Nothing of that sort in
Beckett.']

[note 27] The hieratic language alone turns the radicalism of
existential ontology into a lie. While one confronts nothingness,
while everything is being questioned, the bathos of this questioning
already warrants the meaning it pretends to know nothing about.
The implicit 'nevertheless'. Cryptotheology.
  (Notebook G, p. 117ff.)

[note 28] Take the theological 'unto dust shalt thou return' literally:
filth [*Dreck*], the most intimate, chamber pot, piss, pills are the
universal as remainder. Abstractionism and concretism.
  (Notebook G, p. 119.1)

[321; trans. 150: 'To be sure, the Old Testament saying "You
shall become dust (*Staub*) again" is translated here into "dirt"
(*Dreck*). In the play, the substance of life, a life that is death, is
the excretions.']
[287; trans. 123–24: 'Existential ontology asserts the universally valid in a process of abstraction which is not conscious
of itself. (...) It does so by blotting out particularity – what
is individualized in space and time, what makes existence
existence rather than its mere concept. Ontology appeals to
those who are weary of philosophical formalism but who yet
cling to what is only accessible formally. To such unacknowledged abstraction, Beckett affixes the caustic antithesis by
means of acknowledged subtraction. (...) He lengthens the
escape route of the subject's liquidation to the point where
it constricts into a "this-here," whose abstractness – the loss

of all qualities – extends ontological abstraction literally *ad absurdum* (...)']

[note 29] Homini sapienti sat. Take decadence positively, see p. 112 of this notebook. B[eckett] relates to culture as to a single swarm of Jugendstil ornaments.
(~~Notebook G, p. 119.2~~)

> [284; trans. 121: 'Thoughts are dragged along and distorted like the day's left-overs, *homo homini sapienti sat.*']
> [281; trans. 119: 'Culture parades before him as the entrails of *Jugendstil* ornaments did before that progress which preceded him, modernism as the obsolescence of the modern. The regressive language demolishes it.']

[note 30] The last image is a tableau vivant of a clown, corresponding exactly to the opening scene: with the exception of Clov's possibly decisive travel outfit. Thus it remains open whether it starts all over again or is finished. Berg (Wozzeck!)
(Notebook G, p. 120)

> [314; trans. 145: 'He does manage to make the decision to go, even comes in for the farewell (...) a strong, almost musical conclusion. (...) Aside from some differences, which may be decisive or completely irrelevant, this is identical with the beginning.']
> [316; trans. 146: '(...) whether Clov wins, remains unclear, as if clarity in that would already be too much meaning.']

[note 31] Addition re language. B[eckett]'s progressiveness accords with an idiosyncratic touchiness against modernism. Removal of ornaments. In B[eckett], the objectivity is so hidden that – by removing the meaning – it becomes mysterious and starts to fluoresce.
(~~Notebook G, p. 128ff.~~)

> [281; trans. 119: '(...) modernism as the obsolescence of the modern. The regressive language demolishes it. Such objectivity in Beckett obliterates the meaning that was culture, along with its rudiments. Culture thus begins to fluoresce.']

Translation of Adorno's Notes on *The Unnamable*

1

The 'I' of the beginning and the one at the beginning of the
Recherche

Prolegomena to B[eckett]

Against the 'it can't go on'

Necessity to read each sentence rigorously from beginning
to end

The poem with the outbursts of hatred [i.e. *Whoroscope*]

[In left-hand margin:] see e.g. p. 103 [p. 338 in Calder edition
  of the three novels]
On the situation: absolute alienation is
the absolute subject. But precisely that subject is alienated
from itself, it is the other, it is nothing.
B[eckett]'s novels are the critique of solipsism.
Nothing leads out of this dialectic in his work
At the same time it is the *movens*: the *anything goes*
there is an inherently univocal B[eckett] world, like
Kafka's

[In left-hand margin:] Mahood
B[eckett] reaches the point of indifference between narrative
and theory, just as Marx (and Hegel) wanted
to transform philosophy into history   Completion of the
                                           tendency towards
                                                the reflexive novel
[The word 'novel' is written in the right-hand margin]
Not despairing: schizoid apathy. Not even
able to suffer any more.

The fact that B[eckett] retains the label 'novel'. What has
become of the novel.

something infinitely liberating comes from B[eckett] vis-à-vis
death. What is it?

[The next entry is marked with a vertical line in the left-hand
  margin]

Possibility of interpreting B[eckett] as an attempt
to [respond to] the biblical 'unto dust shalt thou return'. Asking,
   as in the
catechism: What does that mean, 'I am dust'.
Is it consoling that this question is answered?

2

B[eckett]'s deep affinity with music. Like his monologue,
music too always says 'I', but its 'I' too is
always an <u>other</u>, identical and non-identical
at the same time.

The pantheist says: after death I shall be flower, leaf, earth.
B[eckett] puts this to the test: what am I if I am filth [*Dreck*].

B[eckett] as parody of the philosophy of the remainder
   (full of al-
lusions to Descartes). The p[hilosophy of the remainder] says:
   what

                                             remains for me
after the deduction of all costs, surcharges, *trimmings*, advertising as absolute certainty – consciousness as
property, the secret of mineness [*Jemeinigkeit*], which not for nothing sounds like meanness [*Gemeinheit*]. In B[eckett] that
   becomes,
sardonically: how can I <u>ligate</u> everything that exists
   and also
myself? (This is thought in accordance with the capital-
ist market, which B[eckett] takes at its word.)
Answer: by turning myself into a negative
quantity, into <u>less</u> than nothing (filth and
stump are less than a remnant). The sovereign
ego cogitans is transformed by the *dubitatio* into
its opposite. And that is what it always was.
For in order to retain itself as absolutely certain
it had to turn itself into ever less. Sov-
ereignty and filth belong together already in
Kafka; in B[eckett] they become one. The Western
process of subjective reduction calls itself by its
proper name.

There are traces in B[eckett] of an antinomian but
Marcionist theology, like that of God
as a sports fan (in him the Epicurean
gods come into their own). But that too is not to be taken *à
la lettre*, rather as a grimace.
No?

3

B[eckett] has a panic-stricken fear of tape-recordings and
suchlike. And yet he wrote *La Dernière
Bande*. A hole into the work? All that
written as an adjuration: in order not to
have to resemble in any way what is presented? B[eckett] – the
composition of his works proves this – has a very strong
'I'.

The thought of the defensive adjuration and that
of ligation belong immediately together.

From Kafka the most effective motif [is] that of the Hunter
Gracchus. Death, silence, without voices,
as the unattainable goal. Living is dying because it
is a not-being-able-to-die.

The clownish reflections on the work
itself are reminiscent of Gide's *Paludes,* in fact
much is – it is, besides Kafka, the most important
link.

The fellow beings – 'they', the voices – appear
as the absolute negative because they prevent
dying.

The famous metaphysical question: why
is there something and not simply nothing, turns, in
accordance with the form, into something like a Jewish joke:
   You're
right, why on earth is there something and not
simply nothing! ('You're right, Lieutenant,
why should the soldier not cross
the parade ground with a lit cigarette
in his mouth.')

Criticism of B[eckett] amounts to the statement: but all that
is terrible, it simply cannot be. Answer:
it is terrible.

The question of whether the absolutely qualityless point of indifference, which in B[eckett] is the negative, could not
just as well be the positive. But no,
the qualityless, the indeterminate – the
abstract is precisely the negativity.

4
perhaps include the note on nihilism from notebook M

In the light of each new work by B[eckett]
the earlier ones appear simple.

[In left-hand margin:] Difference from Joyce
In B[eckett] there is, as a kind of
counterpoint, something like sound
common sense. Everything
so meaningless, yet at the same time the way one speaks
is so normal, i.e. modern language may have
shrunken – compared with Kafka's epic language, brought as it
    were to
the point of indifference with the absolute subject –
but [it is] never replaced by linguistic absurdity. In that respect
similar to Brecht. Beckett, a Dadaist without Dada.
How my formula of the solipsist without *ipse*
comes into its own in him.

L'innom[*m*]*able* is the negative subject-object

'*Vergammeln*' [To go to seed]. It would be important to know when
    this
word first appeared; index of B[eckett]'s historical significance.
What Beckett does is to compose out this word.

Lukács has observed the emancipation
of time empty of meaning in *L'Éducation sentimentale*. The history
of the novel thereafter is that of the ever more naked emer-
gence of time. With the *monologue intérieur*
it emancipates itself from that which is, from the existent.

As a result, however, time itself disintegrates, already in Proust,
completely in *L'Innom*[*m*]*able*. Absolute time
ceases to be time – just as the Kantian conception of time as pure form cannot be maintained,
because it cannot be represented without
the something of which it is the time [*ein Woran*] (transition to the
   dialectic).
pure *temps durée* turns into
temps espace. That is precisely what occurs in *L'I*[*nnommable*].
The spatial interior is merely space,
proofs of that.

Almost all new art has to pay bitterly for the fact that
it cannot hold out at this point [*auf dem Punkt*]. It cannot
(quote a form). Beckett is the only one who

5
absolutely consistently refuses to go beyond
this point. That is the problem; any jackass
hears the repetition. But that is also precisely his aesthetic task: all that is still possible
at one point.

At the end of the work perhaps: The man who
said one doesn't know whether [one is] living or dead. The
negative truth therein (Kaiser). But
also the contrary, a metaphysics, experience
of a condition beyond death and life
(Kafka!). – No spirits. Indicated
in dreams. What is that.

Perhaps include in the work the notes
taken in Bregenz on nihilism; also a note in an
earlier notebook

Simplest answer to why [*L'Innommable* is] so enormously
   significant:
because it comes closest to the conception of what
it will really be like after death (the *innommable* dreams it).
Neither spirit nor time nor symbol. This is precisely
the Beckettian no man's land. With that the obvious

(the Kafkan moment): the title of the next
book, *Comment c'est*, perhaps suits this one
better.

Archetype of a materialist metaphysics.

The novel is completely unrealistic and at the same time
unauratic.

Against the term 'absurd'. It presupposes
the meaningful as the normal. But that is precisely
the illusion[;] the absurd is the nor-
mal. – That is already manifest in the controversy over '*story*'.

Modern art is the radical heir not only of
avant-garde movements but also
of Naturalism: a disenchanted world, the illu-
sionless, '*comment c'est*'. But

6
Naturalism is still illusionistic in its <u>form</u>,
as though saturated with the toxin of meaning[,] action, etc.
When reading the older naturalists, amaze-
ment at how little naturalist – how badly
stylised they are. B[eckett] gets rid of that, and precisely
in so doing distances himself from the photographic-realist
façade. Naturalism without aura achieves the
aspect which literary criticism then
manipulates as the absurd (NB incommensurability
of Beckett[,] Ionesco and even Camus). In
a second sense, synthesis of radical
Expressionism + Naturalism. – The
disgusting, the decaying [belong to the] *imagery* both of
Naturalism and of Rimbaud.
Supply a theory of the repellent.

Possibility arising from the doctor's gaze. The gaze on
the living from the dissection room. The corpse
as the truth about life, what life <u>becomes</u>, and thus
the terrible equality before which everything that counts,
difference, sinks into irrelevance. Hence
the illnesses, mutilations, excretions as

[7]

the <u>essence</u> of the living. The eccentric is the
rule. Hence also the clown. A living being who
turns himself into an object, thing, football, dead person.

Is nothingness the same as nothing? Everything in B[eckett]
   revolves
around that. Absolute discardment, because there is hope only
where nothing is retained. The fullness
of nothingness. That is the reason for the insistence on the
zero point.

Not abstraction but subtraction

SHANE WELLER

Adorno's Notes on
The Unnamable

Evidence that Adorno valued Beckett's oeuvre above all others
produced in the post-war era is not hard to find. In one of
the paralipomena to his posthumously published *Aesthetic Theory*
(1970), for instance, Adorno places Beckett at the pinnacle of
'contemporary anti-art' (Adorno, 1997, 271), and, as the following
passage in *Negative Dialectics* (1966) makes clear, the value of
Beckett's post-war works lies for Adorno in their being what he
considers the only legitimate response to the Holocaust:

> Beckett has given us the only fitting reaction to the situation of
> the concentration camps – a situation he never calls by name,
> as if it were subject to an image ban. What is, he says, is like a
> concentration camp. At one time he speaks of a lifelong death
> penalty. The only dawning hope is that there will be nothing
> any more. This, too, he rejects. (Adorno, 1973, 380–1)

According to Rolf Tiedemann (the principal editor of his
Gesammelte Schriften), Adorno began reading Beckett in the early

Journal of Beckett Studies 19.2 (2010): 179–195
Edinburgh University Press
DOI: 10.3366/E0309520710000580
© The editors, *Journal of Beckett Studies*
www.eupjournals.com/jobs

1950s, and the first of several meetings between the two men took place in Paris on 28 November 1958, this encounter being memorialised by Adorno in the dedication to Beckett of his 1961 essay on *Endgame*. That essay, placed quite deliberately at the end of the second volume of *Notes to Literature* (1961), is undoubtedly Adorno's major statement on Beckett's art, although important remarks on Beckett are also to be found in the third part of *Negative Dialectics* (1966), in a television discussion on Beckett in which Adorno participated (broadcast on 2 February 1968), and in *Aesthetic Theory*. In each case, the emphasis tends to fall upon Beckett's plays, with *Endgame* receiving particular attention. As a letter of 21 May 1962 from Adorno to the poet and critic Werner Kraft reveals, however, he in fact thought that Beckett's novels, and especially *The Unnamable*, 'surpass even the plays in their significance'. He goes on to inform Kraft that he has just read *The Unnamable* 'with truly feverish interest', and that:

> While reading it, I sketched out an interpretation; perhaps I shall find the time, alongside my major projects, to write it up. But you should definitely read this novel, although strong nerves will be required – in comparison, Kafka's *Penal Colony* is like [Adalbert Stifter's] *Indian Summer*. It is strange that these things in the realm of art have a metaphysical power that their philosophical equivalents – Wittgenstein perhaps, who is clearly an influence on Beckett – seem to me completely to lack; but perhaps you think quite otherwise on the matter. (Adorno, 1994, 34)

As Tiedemann observes, Adorno read *The Unnamable* with pencil in hand, his copy of Elmar Tophoven's German translation – *Der Namenlose* (1959) – containing not only substantial marginalia but also seven pages of notes on the blank pages and the title page at the beginning of the book. Tiedemann reports that, shortly before his death in August 1969, Adorno was still expressing his intention to write an essay on *The Unnamable*, with this essay to be placed at the end of a projected fourth volume of his *Notes to Literature*. Tiedemann describes it as an 'irreparable loss' that Adorno never wrote the essay, even though *Aesthetic Theory* contains some of the major points that would have been made in it (Tiedemann in Adorno, 1994, 22). And yet, for all the importance that Adorno assigns to Beckett's novels – and to *The Unnamable* in particular – in his letter to Kraft, there are very few remarks specifically on the novels in his published works, the most substantial being the following passage in *Aesthetic Theory*:

> [Beckett's] narratives, which he sardonically calls novels, no more offer objective descriptions of social reality than – as the widespread misunderstanding supposes – they present the reduction of life to basic human relationships, that minimum of existence that subsists *in extremis*. These novels do, however, touch on fundamental layers of experience *hic et nunc*, which are brought together into a paradoxical dynamic at a standstill. The narratives are marked as much by an objectively motivated loss of the object as by its correlative, the impoverishment of the subject. Beckett draws the lesson from montage and documentation, from all the attempts to free oneself from the illusion of a subjectivity that bestows meaning. Even where reality finds entry into the narrative, precisely at those points at which reality threatens to suppress what the literary subject once performed, it is evident that there is something uncanny [*nicht geheuer*] about this reality. Its disproportion to the powerless subject, which makes it incommensurable with experience, renders reality unreal [*unwirklicht sie*] with a vengeance. The surplus of reality amounts to its collapse; by striking the subject dead, reality itself becomes deathly; this transition is the artfulness of all antiart, and in Beckett it is pushed to the point of the manifest annihilation of reality. (Adorno, 1997, 30–1)

This statement is very much in line with Adorno's other comments on Beckett's art, however, and raises the question of what difference it would make to substitute the word 'plays' for 'narratives' (*Erzählungen*) or 'novels' in it. As for *The Unnamable*, there are very few explicit comments on that novel in Adorno's published works. In the essay 'Titles' (1962), he asserts that 'One of Beckett's titles, *L'innommable, The Unnamable*, not only fits its subject matter but also embodies the truth about the namelessness of contemporary literature' (Adorno, 1992, 4). In the essay 'Commitment' (1962), he claims that 'Kafka's prose and Beckett's plays and his genuinely colossal [*wahrhaft ungeheuerliche*] novel *The Unnamable* have an effect in comparison to which official works of committed art look like children's games' (Adorno, 1992, 90). And in the paralipomena to *Aesthetic Theory*, he writes:

> The Beckettian zero point–the last straw for a howling philosophy of culture–is, like the atom, infinitely full. It is not inconceivable that humanity would no longer need a closed, immanent culture once it actually had been realized; today, however, the threat is a false destruction of culture, a vehicle of barbarism. The *'Il faut continuer'*, the conclusion of Beckett's *The Unnamable*, condenses this antinomy to its essence: that externally art appears impossible while immanently it must be pursued. (Adorno, 1997, 320)

In each case, one gets little sense of the specificity of *The Unnamable*, of what it is that led Adorno to single it out from Beckett's other post-war works.

According to Tiedemann, if Adorno had written his projected essay on *The Unnamable*, it would have constituted an appendix to *Aesthetic Theory*, evidence in support of one of the key theorems in that work, namely that 'Art is no more able than theory to concretize utopia, not even negatively' (Adorno, 1997, 32; cf. Tiedemann in Adorno, 1994, 74). While this may well be the case, it does not address the question of what the projected essay on *The Unnamable* would have added to Adorno's interpretation of Beckett as articulated in the essay on *Endgame* and the comments in *Aesthetic Theory*, and neither does it address the question of how Adorno might have distinguished between the novels and the plays–and, above all, between *The Unnamable* and *Endgame*. In short, how might Adorno have justified his claim in the letter to Kraft that the novels–and *The Unnamable* in particular–are more significant than the plays? The notes and marginalia in Adorno's copy of the German translation of *The Unnamable* supply an answer–albeit a partial one–to these two questions.

THE PARODY OF PHILOSOPHY

In his notes and marginalia, Adorno engages with a range of philosophical and aesthetic questions, the majority of which are applicable to his interpretation of Beckett's oeuvre as a whole – and, indeed, to his interpretation of modern art more generally – although some do relate specifically to *The Unnamable*. Although the notes are both telegraphic and abstract, the marginalia help to give a sense of the particular passages within the novel that Adorno has in mind for the majority of the topics being addressed. These topics include: the radical alienation of the subject; Beckett's art of reduction (or subtraction), his relation to other writers – above all, to Kafka – and the question of aesthetic form, especially the nature and function of musicality; temporality in the novel after Flaubert, and the heritage of Naturalism and the avant-garde in Beckett's work; the importance of clowning; why it is wrong to apply the concept of the absurd to Beckett; and why an art that locates all hope in death or nothingness can be seen not only to offer the most thoroughgoing critique of the way things are, but also to retain a utopian spirit.

At the heart of Adorno's interpretation of *The Unnamable* is his contention that the novel discloses the fate of the Cartesian subject as a movement towards 'absolute alienation' – the 'I' in Beckett's novel 'is the other, it is nothing'. Countering Georg Lukács' interpretation of Beckett's works as simply expressing solipsism, Adorno sees the novel as 'the critique of solipsism'. The 'dial[ectic] of solipsism' – this phrase being written in the margin beside the lines 'But now, is it I now, I on me? Sometimes I think it is. And then I realise it is not' (Beckett, 1994, 312; Adorno, 1994, 40) – is what, in his essay on *Endgame*, and following Walter Benjamin, Adorno terms the 'dialectic at a standstill' (Adorno, 1982, 149). In his notes on *The Unnamable*, Adorno asserts that the novel takes the 'philosophy of the remainder' (*Residualphilosophie*) at its word. In his essay on *Endgame*, he defines philosophies of the remainder as those philosophies that aim to subtract the temporal and the contingent from life and to retain only that which is 'true and immutable' (Adorno, 1982, 125). In *The Unnamable*, Beckett pursues this reduction to its limit, revealing that it leads not to a self-certain, self-preserving ego, master of itself and its world, but rather to an absolutely alienated subject: 'The sovereign *ego cogitans* is transformed by the *dubitatio* into its opposite. And that is what it always was.' And what that subject always was, according to Adorno, is '<u>less</u> than nothing' or 'filth' (*Dreck*).

In his marginalia, Adorno marks key passages related to this radically alienating reduction of the subject. The sentences 'Nothing then but me, of which I know nothing, except that I have never uttered, and this black, of which I know nothing either, except that it is black, and empty. That then is what, since I have to speak, I shall speak of, until I need speak no more' (306) reveal 'the absolute emptiness of absolute egoity' (Adorno, 1994, 38), while the sentence 'That's suspicious, or rather would be if I still hoped to obtain, from these revelations to come, some truth of more value than those I have been plastered with ever since they took it into their heads I had better exist' (339) is glossed as: 'The absolute I is determined as that which does not exist' (Adorno, 1994, 45). The question of sexuality is also raised when, beside the phrase 'what can be worse than this, a woman's voice perhaps' (367), Adorno writes 'solipsism and homosexuality' (Adorno, 1994, 52). As for the figures of Basil, Mahood and Worm, in marginal notes Adorno identifies Basil as the 'empirical subject', and wonders whether the name might derive from 'basilisk', labels 'Mahood' an 'Aryan name', and then proceeds to identify Mahood as the 'ego' and Worm as the 'id' (Adorno, 1994, 39, 45). In support of this conclusion, he notes in the margin beside the phrase 'what can I say of Worm, who hasn't the wit to make himself plain' (342) that 'the id expresses itself, it does not speak', and beside the lines 'I should have noted them, if only in my head. But Worm cannot note' (342) that 'the id has no memory' (Adorno, 1994, 46).

Overall, Adorno sees Beckett's attitude to Cartesianism and to all philosophies of the remainder as parodic. In the margin beside the lines 'What puzzles me is the thought of being indebted for this information to persons with whom I can never have been in contact. Can it be innate knowledge?' (300), for instance, he writes 'parody of philosophy' (Adorno, 1994, 36), and beside the phrase 'clear and simple notions' (331), he writes: 'Descartes[,] parody of philosophy' (Adorno, 1994, 43). As he clarifies in his essay on *Endgame*, by parody Adorno means 'the use of forms in the epoch of their impossibility' (Adorno, 1982, 136).

In the case of the other major philosopher whose thought Adorno finds in Beckett's novel, however, things are rather different. Although Wittgenstein's name does not appear in the notes, it appears four times in the margins, alongside the following passages: 'I should mention before going any further, any further on, that I say aporia without knowing what it means' (293); 'I have no language but theirs, no, perhaps I'll say it, even with their language, for me alone, so as not to have lived in vain, and so as not to go silent, if that is what confers the right to silence' (328); 'Was geschieht, sind Worte' (Beckett, 2005, 471), translating 'Ce qui se passe, ce sont des mots' (Beckett, 1953, 98), not translated in the English (see Beckett, 1994, 348); and 'Some nice point in semantics, for example, of a nature to accelerate the march of the hours, could not retain my attention' (353) – in this last case, Adorno writing 'W!' in the margin (Adorno, 1994, 49). In each instance, it would appear that Adorno is marking passages that appear to support the claim made in his letter to Kraft that Wittgenstein is an influence on Beckett – something that Beckett himself denied. The parody of philosophy that Adorno finds in *The Unnamable* does not extend, then, to Wittgenstein.

A LITERATURE BEYOND KAFKA?

While Adorno's reading of *The Unnamable* is a philosophical one – taking the novel as a critique of solipsism and a parody of the philosophy of the remainder – he also aims to situate Beckett within a literary context and to consider some of the major formal aspects of the novel. As I have sought to demonstrate elsewhere (see Weller, 2009), Adorno's interpretation of Beckett involves the generalisation of a principle of indifferentiation, with the distinction between philosophy and literature being one of the key distinctions to be affected by this principle. In his notes on *The Unnamable*, Adorno asserts that Beckett reaches 'the point of indifference between narrative and theory', although he wishes to retain a sense of the radical specificity of the literary, arguing in the 1968 television discussion that 'literary solipsism is something quite different from philosophical solipsism' (Adorno, 1994, 109). In his notes on *The Unnamable*, Adorno refers explicitly to Proust,

Kafka, Gide, Joyce, Brecht, Flaubert, Kaiser, Ionesco, Camus, and Rimbaud, as well as to various artistic movements (Naturalism, Expressionism, and Dada). In his marginal notes, the names Brecht, Joyce, Valéry, and Gertrude Stein all appear once, Gottfried Benn twice, and Kafka fourteen times.

The two passages that lead Adorno to think of Gottfried Benn – author of the 1912 collection *Morgue and Other Poems* – are 'it's like slime' (367; Adorno, 1994, 52) and 'the charge is sounded, present arms, corpse, to your guns, spermatozoon' (382; Adorno, 1994, 55). Although not named, Benn is also no doubt in Adorno's mind when, towards the end of the notes, he remarks on the 'Possibility arising from the doctor's gaze. The gaze on the living from the dissection room. The corpse as the truth about life, what life becomes'. As for Paul Valéry, it is the phrase 'the murmurs of olden silences' (369; Adorno, 1994, 52) that prompts Adorno to think of the poet. In the case of Stein, it is the use of repetition, as in the line 'They'll clap me in a dungeon, I'm in a dungeon, I've always been in a dungeon' (372; Adorno, 1994, 53). The mention of Gide's *Paludes* in the notes, in relation to the 'clownish reflections on the work itself', is significant not least because it leads on to the mention of Kafka. In a footnote to his 1953 essay on Kafka, Adorno remarks that Gide 'would have remained the author of "Paludes", had he not made the mistake of attempting to do *The Trial'* (Adorno, 1981, 263). Unlike Gide, Beckett does not – as Adorno sees it – attempt to imitate Kafka, although Kafka remains by far the most important literary point of reference. Kafka's name appears far more than any other in the marginalia, and seven passages in the notes relate Beckett to him.

Among the brief notes taken by Adorno after his first meeting with Beckett in November 1958, there is the following: 'with B[eckett] until very late. Spoke very seriously. His objections to Kafka' (Adorno, 1994, 23). As Adorno reveals in the 1968 television discussion, those objections were essentially the same as the ones made in conversation with Israel Shenker in 1956 and in letters to Hans Neumann on 17 February 1954 and to Ruby Cohn on 17 January 1962. To Shenker, Beckett remarked that 'Kafka's form is classic, it goes on like a steamroller – almost serene' (Beckett in Graver and Federman, 1979, 148). As Adorno understood the matter, Beckett was convinced that the form of Kafka's works remains undisturbed by its content – and that Kafka is 'still too realist in his linguistic form' (Adorno, 1994, 93).

In his essay on Kafka, Adorno anticipates Beckett's characterisation of Kafka's prose as classic in its serenity, but does not see this as a failing: 'There is', he writes, 'nothing mad in [Kafka's] prose, unlike the writer from whom he learned decisively, Robert Walser; every sentence has been shaped by a mind in full control of itself; yet, at the same time, every sentence has been snatched from the zone of insanity into which all knowledge must venture if it is to become such in an age when sound common sense only reinforces universal blindness' (Adorno, 1981, 253–4). As for *The Unnamable*, in his notes Adorno characterises the novel as 'completely unrealistic and at the same time unauratic', and also highlights what he takes to be Beckett's 'deep affinity with music'. Schönberg's name appears once in the margin and Stravinsky's twice, the most important of these associations being that of Stravinsky with the sentence: 'Overcome, that goes without saying, the fatal leaning towards expressiveness' (394; Adorno, 1994, 58). As for the place of music more generally, in the margin beside the line 'They say he hears them, they don't know, perhaps he does, yes, he hears, nothing else is certain' (361), Adorno writes: 'Worm hears. Enormous significance [*Ungeheuere Bedeutung*] of the voice. Relation to the musical' (Adorno, 1994, 51). For a clarification of what Adorno understands by the musicality of Beckett's prose, one has to turn to his remarks on the matter in the 1968 television discussion. There, he argues that Beckett's musicality lies not in any linguistic imitation of musical effects of the kind to be found in the poetry of Rilke and Swinburne, but rather in the way in which linguistic sounds 'are organised into structures' such that 'The prose is not simply organised by meaning' (Adorno, 1994, 96–7). As he observes in the notes on *The Unnamable*, Adorno finds a similarity between the Beckettian monologue and music in that the latter 'too always says "I", but its "I" too is always an other, identical and non-identical at the same time'. Furthermore, when identifying Beckett's historical significance, Adorno relies on the Austrian music theorist Heinrich Schenker's concept of 'composing out' (*Auskomponierung*). According to Schenker, most eighteenth- and nineteenth-century music can be understood as the 'composing out' of fundamental structures (*Ursätze*). Adorno sees

Beckett as 'composing out' the word *vergammeln*, meaning 'to go to seed', or 'to go bad'.

Characterised by its musical structure, its use of repetition, its being a 'shrunken' language that never lapses into 'linguistic absurdity', *The Unnamable* requires, according to Adorno, a reading that is 'rigorous' in its movement from the beginning to the end of each sentence. Such a reading process is, of course, particularly demanding in the case of *The Unnamable*, Adorno himself noting that 'the long sentence seems to begin here' in the margin beside the line 'Well, I prefer that, I must say I prefer that' (385; Adorno, 1994, 55) and underlining the full stop after 'I see nothing else, I see nothing whatever, for the time being' (393) and writing in the margin 'the long sentence ends here' (Adorno, 1994, 57). Towards the end of the novel, he also identifies examples of what he terms 'model sentences' (*Mustersätze*). These include 'I must feel something, yes, I feel something, they say I feel something, I don't know what it is, I don't know what I feel' (386; Adorno, 1994, 56), which suggests that the kind of sentence Adorno has in mind begins by positing something and then proceeds to undo it through a form of *correctio* leading to the expression of radical unknowing. Despite Beckett's own objection to Kafka's prose style, such model sentences bear a striking resemblance to Kafka's own late style, as in the unfinished story 'The Burrow', to which Adorno refers in a marginal note beside the line 'That must be something, while waiting for oblivion, to feel a prop and buckler, not only for one of one's six planes, but for two, for the first time' (360; Adorno, 1994, 51).

In his essay on *Endgame*, Adorno describes that play as 'heir to Kafka's novels', and goes on to characterise Beckett's relation to Kafka as similar to that of the serial composers to Schönberg, by which he means that Beckett 'reflects the precursor [Kafka] in himself, altering the latter through the totality of his principle. Beckett's critique of the earlier writer, which irrefutably stresses the divergence between what happens and the objectively pure, epic language, conceals the same difficulty as that confronted by contemporary integral composition with the antagonistic procedure of Schönberg' (Adorno, 1982, 136). A similar characterisation of Kafka's language is to be found in Adorno's notes on *The Unnamable*. As for the claim that Beckett alters Kafka 'through the totality of his principle' (*krempelt ihm um durch Totalität seines*

Prinzips), many of the points made in Adorno's essay on Kafka are in fact simply repeated in his reading of Beckett. The claim made in the 1953 essay that in Kafka one finds a 'completely estranged subjectivity' (Adorno, 1981, 261) is, as we have seen, one of Adorno's core theses on *The Unnamable*. Just as he remarks on Kafka's affinity with 'antinomian mysticism' in the 1953 essay (Adorno, 1981, 268), so he writes 'antinomian theology' (Adorno, 1994, 46) in the margin of *The Unnamable* beside the line 'The essential is to go on squirming forever at the end of the line, as long as there are waters and banks and ravening in heaven a sporting God to plague his creature, per pro his chosen shits' (341), and, in the notes, asserts that 'There are traces in B[eckett] of an antinomian but Marcionist theology, like that of God as a sports fan'. In his notes, Adorno links this theology to the philosophy of Epicurus, this connection being clarified by his writing 'Epicurus' in the margin beside the phrase 'No spectator then, and better still no spectacle, good riddance' (378; Adorno, 1994, 54). In *Minima Moralia* (1951), Adorno describes Kafka as 'the solipsist without ipseity' (Adorno, 1978, 223), and, in the notes on *The Unnamable*, one finds: 'How my formula of the solipsist without *ipse* comes into its own in him [Beckett]'. In the margin beside the passage beginning 'But do I roll, in the manner of a true ball?' (308), he writes 'Kafka' (Adorno, 1994, 38), Tiedemann suggesting that Adorno is probably thinking here of Kafka's story 'The Cares of a Family Man', in the collection *A Country Doctor* (1919). That short text describes a strange being named 'Odradek' who looks like a 'flat star-shaped spool' but is animate, and about whom the narrator asks: 'Can he possibly die? Anything that dies has had some kind of aim in life, some kind of activity, which has worn out; but that does not apply to Odradek' (Kafka, 1993, 183–4). Another passage in *The Unnamable* – 'but there it is, that is the way to speak of him, that is the way to speak to him, as if he were alive, as if he could understand, as if he could desire, even if it serves no purpose, and it serves none' (361) – is explicitly marked 'Odradek' (Adorno, 1994, 51).

   In his essay on Kafka, Adorno connects Odradek with a figure in one of Kafka's posthumously published fragments, the Hunter Gracchus, who has died but whose 'death ship lost its way', such that he remains a perpetual wanderer on earth (Kafka, 1993, 368). According to Adorno, Odradek and Gracchus may be thought together because 'The zone in which it is impossible to die is also the no-man's-land between man and thing' (Adorno, 1981, 263). In the same essay, he connects Gracchus both with the fate of the bourgeoisie – which 'failed to die' – and with the experience of prisoners in the Nazi concentration camps:

> In the concentration camps, the boundary between life and death was eradicated. A middleground was created, inhabited by living skeletons and putrefying bodies, victims unable to take their own lives, Satan's laughter at the hope of abolishing death. As in Kafka's twisted epics, what perished there was that which had provided the criterion of experience – life lived out to its end. Gracchus is the consummate refutation of the possibility banished from the world: to die after a long and full life. (Adorno, 1981, 260)

As noted at the beginning of the present essay, in *Negative Dialectics* Adorno makes a similar argument for Beckett's work in general, in which one finds existence being presented as 'like a concentration camp' (Adorno, 1973, 380). According to Adorno, that is what makes Beckett's work genuinely historical and political. He then goes on to note that 'At one time [Beckett] speaks of a lifelong death penalty [*von lebenslanger Todesstrafe*]' (Adorno, 1973, 380–1). The marginalia in *The Unnamable* reveal that the 'one time' of which Adorno is thinking here occurs in that novel, the note 'Loujche condemned to a lifelong death penalty [*lebenslänglicher Todesstrafe*]' (Adorno, 1994, 51) appearing in the margin beneath 'And it is a blessing for him [Worm] he cannot stir, even though he suffers because of it, for it would be to sign his life-warrant [*Lebensurteil*]' (361). As Tiedemann explains, 'Loujche' is a parodied diminutive of the Frankfurt dialect form of the French name 'Louis', Adorno here referring to a remark made by his uncle Louis Prosper Calvelli-Adorno (1866–1960). This idea of life as a death penalty fits with another passage in Beckett's novel that leads Adorno to write 'Kafka' in the margins, the passage in question concerning the idea that there is a 'pensum' (*Strafarbeit*) that has to be discharged before the narrator can fall silent (see Beckett, 1994, 312–13).

In his notes on *The Unnamable*, Adorno states that the 'simplest answer' to the question of why that novel is 'so enormously significant' (*so ungeheuer bedeutend*) is that 'it comes closest to the conception of what it will really be like after death'. However, as is made clear by a marginal note beside the line 'But say I succeed in dying, to adopt the most comfortable hypothesis, without having been able to believe I ever lived, I know to my cost it is not that they wish for me' (344), Adorno sees the 'Beckettian no man's land' as being located not literally 'after death', but rather in a 'realm between life and death' (Adorno, 1994, 47). That no man's land (*Niemandsland*) is inhabited by a being whose existence is unbearable and yet who is not permitted to die: in the margin beside the line 'I see my place, there is nothing to show it, nothing to distinguish it, from all the other places, they are mine, all mine' (367), Adorno writes: 'They – that is, human beings – want him to live [...] and it is their fault that his existence itself is a fault [*und das ist ihre Schuld an ihm wie Dasein selber Schuld ist*]' (Adorno, 1994, 52). Adorno sees this conception of existence as a *Schuld* – fault, debt, sin, offence – as an important connection between Beckett and Kafka: in a marginal note, he writes that Beckett 'shares with Kafka the idea of existence as fault [*Schuld*]' (Adorno, 1994, 46). If the Hunter Gracchus is the 'most effective motif' to come from Kafka, that is because it figures 'Death, silence, without voices, as the unattainable goal' for the being whose existence is such a *Schuld*.

NIHILISM AND UTOPIA

Given that Adorno takes the essential similarity between Beckett and Kafka to be their presentation of existence as an offence for which one is condemned to a suffering without end (since death is impossible), it might seem reasonable to assume that he sees their works simply as expressions of nihilism, and, on two occasions in his notes on *The Unnamable*, Adorno does flag the possibility of including material on nihilism from his other notebooks (Tiedemann observes that the material in question has not been identified). In this regard, the key concept becomes that of hope, and on this matter Adorno finds Beckett inverting Kafka. To Beckett's line 'While there's life there's hope' (336), Adorno responds with the marginal note: '!!! This is the worst [*das Äußerste*]'

(Adorno, 1994, 44), and then, in the margin beside the lines 'Is there then no hope? Good gracious, no, heavens, what an idea! Just a faint one perhaps, but which will never serve' (369), he writes: 'orthodox Kafka. But inverted: for here nothingness is the hope' (Adorno, 1994, 53). Adorno is probably alluding here to a remark made by Kafka in conversation with Max Brod on 28 February 1920, and recorded in Brod's 1937 biography of Kafka, that there is 'Plenty of hope – for God – no end of hope – only not for us' (Brod, 1947, 61). In his essay on Kafka, however, Adorno claims that 'To include him among the pessimists, the existentialists of despair, is as misguided as to make him a prophet of salvation' (Adorno, 1981, 269). Similarly, in the section on nihilism in *Negative Dialectics* he distinguishes Beckett from the nihilists – by which, paradoxically, he means those who 'oppose nihilism with their more and more faded positivities' (Adorno, 1973, 381).

If neither Kafka nor Beckett is an existentialist of despair, if neither is a nihilist in Lukács' sense of the term, this is not because they offer any alternative to the horror of modernity. Rather, their resistance to that world is articulated *in the negative*. As Adorno puts it in *Negative Dialectics*: 'To Beckett, as to the Gnostics, the created world is radically evil, and its negation is the chance of another world that is not yet. As long as the world is as it is, all pictures of reconciliation, peace, and quiet resemble the picture of death' (Adorno, 1973, 381). Adorno finds precisely such pictures of death in *The Unnamable*. At the bottom of the page ending (in the German) 'But the other voice, of him who does not share this passion for the animal kingdom' (338), he writes: 'in B[eckett], the positive categories, such as hope, are the absolutely negative ones. Hope is directed towards nothingness' (Adorno, 1994, 44). As he argues in the 1968 television discussion, it is in their conviction that 'hope is to be sought only in figures of death or in figures of nothingness' that Adorno finds the 'deep elective affinity' between Beckett and another writer of the post-Holocaust period, the poet Paul Celan (Adorno, 1994, 114).

The locating of hope in figures of nothingness entails an aesthetics of radical reduction – a writing of the negative that is subtractive rather than abstracting. In his essay on Kafka, Adorno describes Kafka's work as a 'demolition' – 'He tears down the soothing façade to which a repressive reason increasingly conforms' (Adorno, 1981, 252). In *The Unnamable,* he finds a similar process of demolition, with the subject being reduced to filth (*Dreck*), to *less* than nothing, and with time being reduced to space. As becomes clear at the end of his notes, however, Adorno sees this demolition as orientated towards a highly paradoxical nothingness in Beckett's novel: 'Absolute discardment, because there is hope only where nothing is retained. The fullness of nothingness. That is the reason for the insistence on the zero point.' This Beckettian zero point (*Nullpunkt*) has to be understood, then, as a fullness, or, as Adorno puts it in the television discussion, as a 'positive nothingness' or '*nihil relativum*' – as 'the negation of something that exists' (Adorno, 1994, 82). According to Adorno, all Beckett's artistic energy revolves around this point, and *The Unnamable* stands out precisely on account of its unqualified commitment to this 'aesthetic <u>task</u>'. And yet, Adorno insists, the guarantor of the value of this nothingness is its impossibility. While Beckett bears obvious affinities with Schopenhauer, the crucial difference between them is that Beckett does not accept that the denial of the will to live is possible (see Adorno, 1994, 104). So it is that Beckett's writing of the negative in *The Unnamable* is in fact a writing of the *failure* of the negative, but a failure that never results in the abandonment of the task at hand. In his marginalia, Adorno emphasises this point by underlining 'go on' (*weitermachen*) twice in the phrase 'on the purpose to be achieved, and simply go on, with no illusion about having begun one day or ever being able to conclude' (388) – in the German, *weitermachen* occurs twice, as does *continuer* in the French (see Beckett, 2005, 525; 1953, 163) – and noting in the margin: 'Going on is a major category. And a <u>critical</u> one: against the deception of the question of meaning' (Adorno, 1994, 56).

Although he does not refer to the concept of the ethical, one may argue that Adorno considers *The Unnamable* to be an ethical work in at least three, interrelated senses. First, as he makes clear in the 1968 television discussion, 'the moral element' lies in Beckett's disclosure of the fact that the subject, the 'I', is not the ultimate: it is 'valueless' (*nichtig*) and mediated (Adorno, 1994, 118). Secondly, the novel locates utopia in an impossible death or nothingness: as Adorno argues in *Aesthetic Theory,* this is not nihilism, but rather a recognition that 'Art is no more able than theory to concretize utopia, not even negatively [. . .]; only by virtue of the absolute negativity of collapse does art enunciate the unspeakable: utopia' (Adorno, 1997, 32). And thirdly, despite the unattainability of this utopia, Beckett insists on the need to 'go on', reducing ever further, 'because there is hope only where nothing is retained'.

There is, however, one more way in which Beckett's novel might be seen as ethical in Adorno's terms. In his essay on *Endgame*, Adorno argues that the play ends in such a way that 'No spectator and no philosopher can say if the play will not begin anew. The dialectic swings to a standstill' (Adorno, 1982, 145). In *The Unnamable*, he finds hermeneutic openness in the very conception of nothingness, asking on the last page of his notes: 'Is nothingness the same as nothing [*Ist das Nichts gleich nichts*]?', and adding: 'Everything in B[eckett] revolves around that.' In other words, Adorno sees Beckett leaving open the question of whether or not utopia does lie in nothingness. But if that openness can be seen to ensure the novel's ethical nature, it also allows nihilism – as the thought that perhaps *das Nichts* is simply *nichts* – to haunt Beckett's novel in a way that the ethicalising reading cannot exorcise, since that reading would not be possible other than by opening the door to nihilism.

To return, finally, to the two questions with which we began: Adorno's notes and marginalia on *The Unnamable* are undoubtedly a valuable addition to his other reflections on Beckett's oeuvre, and it is certainly to be regretted that the projected essay on the novel was never written. On the evidence of these notes, it would seem that in *The Unnamable* Adorno finds a prose that accomplishes a more radical decomposition of the subject than is to be found in any other work of literature with which Adorno was familiar, including *Endgame*. His remarks on the novel place it at the end of a long aesthetic tradition: the 'I' has been completely alienated and reduced to filth, time has been reduced to space, the distinction between narrative and theory has been collapsed, an entire philosophical tradition has been subjected to withering critique, and the horror of modernity has been disclosed. And yet, Adorno concludes, in Beckett's art of subtraction the hope of a better world survives, if only in a nothingness that might not – just might not – coincide with itself.

WORKS CITED

Adorno, Theodor W. (1973), *Negative Dialectics*, trans. E. B. Ashton, London: Routledge & Kegan Paul.

Adorno, Theodor W. (1978), *Minima Moralia: Reflections from Damaged Life*, trans. E. F. N. Jephcott, London: Verso.

Adorno, Theodor W. (1981), *Prisms*, trans. Samuel and Shierry Weber, Cambridge, MA: The MIT Press.

Adorno, Theodor W. (1982), 'Trying to Understand *Endgame*', trans. Michael T. Jones, *New German Critique* 26: *Critical Theory and Modernity* (Spring-Summer 1982), pp. 119–150.

Adorno, Theodor W. (1991), *Notes to Literature*, vol. 1, ed. Rolf Tiedemann, trans. Shierry Weber Nicholsen, New York: Columbia University Press.

Adorno, Theodor W. (1992), *Notes to Literature*, vol. 2, ed. Rolf Tiedemann, trans. Shierry Weber Nicholsen, New York: Columbia University Press.

Adorno, Theodor W. (1994), *Frankfurter Adorno Blätter III*, ed. Theodor W. Adorno Archiv, Munich: edition text + kritik.

Adorno, Theodor W. (1997), *Aesthetic Theory*, ed. Gretel Adorno and Rolf Tiedemann, trans. Robert Hullot-Kentor, London: Athlone.

Beckett, Samuel (1953), *L'Innommable*, Paris: Les Éditions de Minuit.

Beckett, Samuel (1994), *Molloy, Malone Dies, The Unnamable*, London: Calder Publications.

Beckett, Samuel (2005), *Drei Romane. Molloy. Malone stirbt. Der Namenlose*, Frankfurt am Main: Suhrkamp.

Brod, Max (1947), *The Biography of Franz Kafka*, trans. G. Humphreys Roberts, London: Secker & Warburg.

Graver, Lawrence, and Raymond Federman, eds. (1979), *Samuel Beckett: The Critical Heritage*, London: Routledge & Kegan Paul.

Kafka, Franz (1993), *Collected Stories*, ed. Gabriel Josipovici, New York: Alfred A. Knopf.

Weller, Shane (2009), 'The Art of Indifference: Adorno's Manuscript Notes on *The Unnamable*', in Daniela Guardamagna and Rossana M. Sebellin (eds), *The Tragic Comedy of Samuel Beckett: 'Beckett in Rome', 17–19 April 2008*, Rome: Laterza: 223–37.

DIRK VAN HULLE

Adorno's Notes on *Endgame*

1.

Theodor W. Adorno's essay 'Versuch, das Endspiel zu verstehen' is part of his collection of essays *Noten zur Literatur*. The choice to present his interpretation of *Endgame* as an attempt (an essay in the literal sense of *un essai*) is linked to the decision to regard all his essays on literature as mere 'notes'. To try and understand (*verstehen*) this interest in the nature of the 'note', it seems suitable to start with his expertise as a musicologist. After graduating in Frankfurt, where he studied philosophy, musicology, psychology and sociology, he went to Vienna in 1925 and made contacts with Arnold Schönberg and members of the Viennese School. Twenty years later, this firsthand knowledge of Schönberg's twelve-tone technique was appealed to by Thomas Mann, during the writing of *Doktor Faustus* – probably the most complex and profound novel about Germany and the Germans ever written. Mann thematised the vexing question of how the country of Bach, Beethoven, Goethe and Dürer had allowed itself to turn into a fascist state of terror. He did so by means of the fictitious composer Adrian

Journal of Beckett Studies 19.2 (2010): 196–217
Edinburgh University Press
DOI: 10.3366/E0309520710000592
© The editors, *Journal of Beckett Studies*
www.eupjournals.com/jobs

Leverkühn, who enters into a Faustian pact for creative genius. By contracting syphilis he deepens his inspiration, resulting in extraordinary musical creativity that finds its expression in twelve-tone compositions à la Arnold Schönberg.

The most difficult part in the writing of *Doktor Faustus*, however, was the (literary) creation of Leverkühn's musical compositions. In this respect, Adorno acted as the novelist's adviser. To 'compose' his protagonist's symphonic cantata 'Doktor Fausti Weheklag' Mann needed all the musicological advice he could get from Adorno. Afterwards, in his account of the 'making-of' (*Die Entstehung des Doktor Faustus*), he did acknowledge Adorno's role in this twelve-tone composition, but he failed to mention a few important details (which he had originally included in his draft, but later omitted; transcription in Voss, 197). For instance, it was Adorno who came up with the idea of taking the twelve-syllable sentence 'Denn ich sterbe als ein böser und guter Christ' as the general theme of the composition.

The twelve syllables served as the verbal expression of a musical tone row. As opposed to traditional compositions, implying a hierarchy in which all notes related to the dominant, Leverkühn's music started from this tone row or motif of twelve notes, none of which was more important than the others. Thus, atonality did away with musical hierarchy. Nonetheless, Adorno had some reservations. Undoing this hierarchy may have been a laudable principle in and of itself, but this process was driven to such extremes that it became a totalising system. As Evelyn Cobley notes, 'Adorno was particularly sensitive to the dangerous implications of Schönberg's dismantling of the key system. (…) While providing insights into the illusory pretences of the closed bourgeois work, the twelve-tone composition does not recognize its own suspect ideological investments and mystifications. It is in the attempt to eliminate the last vestiges of hierarchy that the serial system becomes totalitarian' (Cobley, 187–8). After having introduced contingency by means of atonality, Schönberg – according to Adorno's analysis – was intimidated by its potential anarchy and consequently tried to contain it in a strict serial system.

Adorno explained this musicological theory to Mann in the first week of January 1946, in Pacific Palisades (California), where they

were both living in exile. Mann went to Adorno's with his notebook
('zu Adorno mit Notizbuch', he writes in his diary on 6 January
1946) and jotted numerous ideas, which he then 'fixed' (*befestigte*)
in his so-called 'Notizenkonvolut' (Mann qtd. in Voss, 1975, 188):
'There would no longer be any free note' (*Es gäbe keine freie Note
mehr*) is one of the crucial sentences in these notes, summarising
the paradox of the complicity between contingency and strict
form (*strenger Satz*) that is so central in *Doktor Faustus*. The total
integration of twelve-tone technique is generated under the guise
of liberation from hierarchy.

Adorno's sensitivity to this totalising aspect of Schönberg's
twelve-tone technique is reflected in his decision to present
his ideas on literature as simply 'notes' ('Aufzeichnungen zu
Kafka', *Noten zur Literatur*). Notes are usually non-hierarchical –
a characteristic they have in common with Schönberg's twelve-tone
music – but in Adorno's case they also crucially lack the totalising
aspect. Therefore it is fortunate, and perhaps not a coincidence,
that Adorno has preserved his reflections on *L'Innommable* and *Fin
de partie* in the form of notes, admirably made accessible by Rolf
Tiedemann (1994). Consequently, it seems appropriate to discuss
these notes in the form of notes – not twelve, though, as in the
strict form of Leverkühn's twelve-tone compositions, but a more
Beckettian number.

2.

On 29 February 1961, Samuel Beckett was invited by the head of
Suhrkamp Verlag, Siegfried Unseld, to have lunch with Theodor
W. Adorno. On this occasion, the author of the essay 'Versuch,
das Endspiel zu verstehen' insisted on making a link between
Endgame's protagonist Hamm and Shakespeare's Hamlet, even
though Beckett explicitly told him he had never thought of
Hamlet when he invented Hamm's name. Apparently Beckett
even became 'a little angry' during this conversation over lunch,
which took place on the same day as the celebration in Beckett's
honour, organised by Suhrkamp and programmed that evening
in the Kantate-Saal next to the Goethe-Haus. James Knowlson has
provided the details of this encounter, based on Unseld's address to

the second international Beckett symposium in The Hague (8 April 1992): 'In the evening Adorno started his speech and, of course, pointed out the derivation of "Hamm" from "Hamlet"', in reaction to which Beckett whispered in Unseld's ear what is translated and passed on as 'This is the progress of science that professors can proceed with their errors!' (qtd. in Knowlson, 479).

3.

As a consequence of this account, Adorno tends to be better known in Beckett studies as the 'crritic' who failed to listen to Beckett than as the sociologist/philosopher/musicologist who drew attention to the difference between Beckett's work and existentialism. After all, the reference to Hamlet in his essay 'Versuch, das Endspiel zu verstehen' is only a relatively insignificant passage, compared to the wealth of reflections in the rest of the essay. By translating Adorno's essay into English (1982), Michael T. Jones has played an important role in its reception in the Anglophone world, and possibly the relevant Hamlet passage in his translation has also had an influence on this reception:

> das Verenden der beiden Alten [treibt] vorwärts zu jenem Aus-gang des Lebens, dessen Möglichkeit das Spannungsmoment bildet. Hamlet wird variiert: Krepieren oder Krepieren, das ist hier die Frage. Den Namen des Shakespeareschen Helden kürzt grimmig der des Beckettschen ab, der des liquidierten dramatischen Subjekts den des ersten. (Adorno, 1981, 312)

> the old pair's miserable end drives it [the main plot] forward to that exit of life whose possibility constitutes the tension of the play. Hamlet is revised: croak or croak, that is the question. The name of Shakespeare's hero is grimly foreshortened by Beckett – the last, liquidated dramatic subject echoing the first. (Adorno, 1982, 143)

What Adorno presented as a variation on a theme ('a variation on Hamlet' in Shierry Weber Nicholsen's translation, 1991, 267) became a revision in Jones's translation, and whereas Adorno wrote that Hamm's name grimly foreshortens or abbreviates

Hamlet's, the translation added the notion of echoing. This echo may create the impression of 'the neatness of identifications' (1984, 19) against which Beckett already warned in his early critical work. Steven Connor connects Adorno's Hamm/Hamlet link with this opening line of 'Dante... Bruno.Vico..Joyce' (Connor, 2010). Adorno's notes on *Endgame* enable us to judge how 'neat' this identification is.

The first reference to Hamlet in 'Versuch, das Endspiel zu verstehen' serves to illustrate a principle Adorno discerns in Beckett's dramatic strategies. The formulation of this principle is drafted as follows in [note 2]:

An old man takes a nap and pulls a handkerchief over his eyes. Completely harmless in natural life: the horror that emanates from it when isolated in a tableau vivant. B[eckett]'s method consists in releasing such situations and their expression, turning them into a second, autonomous context.

In the published version of the essay, Adorno refers to the actors' scene in *Hamlet* (Adorno, 1982, 132) as an example of a situation from which the horror emanates because it is isolated from its real-life occurrence. Adorno refers to Shakespeare (not so much as an identification, but 'perhaps as a reminiscence'), but in the notes he connects the same method, on the one hand, to Schönberg and twelve-tone music and, on the other hand, to Kafka, notably 'Beckett's criticism of Kafka' [note 2].

Adorno does not specify what this criticism consisted of, but Rolf Tiedemann convincingly suggests that it may correspond to what Adorno claimed in this context during a TV broadcast (2 February 1968, Westdeutsches Fernsehen WDR). During this discussion with Walter Boehlich, Martin Esslin, Hans-Geert Falkenberg and Ernst Fischer, Adorno mentioned that Beckett was critical of Kafka because – from the perspective of linguistic form – the latter's work was still too realistic (Adorno et al., 1994, 93). This background colours the other reference to Shakespeare in the essay, relating Hamm to Hamlet (1982, 143), for the identification is at least complicated by Kafkaesque and Schönbergian elements in the 'Hamlet' amalgam he seems to have had in mind when he made the reference to Shakespeare. Adorno's idea of Hamlet was undoubtedly somewhat different from Beckett's, and the identification therefore less neat than the one Beckett objected to when Adorno repeated the allusion in his lecture.

4.

The account of the meeting between Beckett and Adorno in Frankfurt naturally raises the question why Adorno did not simply omit the passage. But it also makes one wonder why Beckett insisted on the denial of this reference. He must have realised that – at least since T. S. Eliot's 'Tradition and the Individual Talent' and especially in the critical climate shortly after Wimsatt and Beardsley's essay 'The Intentional Fallacy' (1954) – the objection that he, as the author of *Fin de partie*, had never thought of Hamlet when he invented Hamm's name was perhaps not the most convincing argument to talk Adorno out of alluding to Shakespeare in his lecture. As a consequence, his anger seems to hide other concerns.

In a previous phase of Beckett's writing career, notably during the extremely creative period shortly after the Second World War, Hamlet did play a role in his writing – as did other incarnations of the contemplation of suicide, such as Gloucester and Faust. For instance, when the narrator in *Premier amour* (written between 28 October and 12 November 1946) considers that to be omnidolent would simplify matters considerably and admits that he does not understand his pains sufficiently, he concludes: 'Cela doit venir de ce que je ne suis pas que douleur. Voilà l'astuce.' (Beckett, 1970, 24) That Beckett may have had in mind Hamlet's 'heartache and the thousand natural shocks / That flesh is heir to' (1997, 1705; Act III, scene I) seems to be confirmed by his 1971 translation of the story: 'That must come from my not being all pain and nothing else. There's the rub' (Beckett, 1995, 32) – alluding to Hamlet's 'rub': 'To die, to sleep. / To sleep, perchance to dream. Ay, there's the rub' (1997, 1705; Act III, scene I).

When, two years after writing *Premier amour*, Beckett was working on his play *En attendant Godot* (between 9 October 1948 and 29 January 1949) in the notebook preserved at the Bibliothèque Nationale de France, the contemplation of suicide became the subcutaneous subject of an eight-page scene that was later omitted. Colin Duckworth visited Beckett in April 1965 and had only a few hours to study this manuscript. In his notes he mentions a long passage that did not make it into the published version of the play – a long dialogue concerning the question 'Est-ce que c'est la peine' ('Is it worthwhile'). But the circumstances did not allow him to transcribe the whole passage (Duckworth, 34).

In the published text of *En attendant Godot*, just before Didi and Gogo 'do the tree' in the second act (Beckett, 1990, 71; 1996, 107), they first abuse each other and then make up again. Whereas the English version is quite explicit – the curses ranging from 'Moron' to 'Crritic' – the stage directions in the French text simply mention an '*Échange d'injures*' (106). The occasion of this exchange is an unfinished sentence. Gogo first says 'They're coming!' (68) But nobody comes. Didi and Gogo start watching, but they do not see anything, so Didi concludes: 'You must have had a vision' (69). They resume their watch in silence, and then suddenly start asking themselves a question:

> Vladimir & Estragon: [*Turning simultaneously.*] Do you –
> Vladimir: Oh, pardon!
> Estragon: Carry on.
> Vladimir: No no, after you.
> Estragon: No no, you first.
> Vladimir: I interrupted you.
> Estragon: On the contrary.
> [*They glare at each other angrily.*] (Beckett, 1990, 70)

In the Minuit edition the question they both ask simultaneously is:

> Vladimir & Estragon: Est-ce...
> Vladimir: Oh pardon!
> Estragon: Je t'écoute.
> Vladimir: Mais non!
> Estragon: Mais si!
> Vladimir: Je t'ai coupé.
> Estragon: Au contraire.
> *Ils se regardent avec colère.*

What ensues in the manuscript is a nonsensical exchange of what Adorno called 'protocol sentences' (Adorno, 1982, 137) – a conversation in the same vein as the one above, but twenty times as long. It brings to a head what Adorno later noted with regard to *Endgame*: 'There is something absurd in the form of the dialogue itself; meaninglessness of the question-and-answer relationship' [note 8]. The nonsensical character of the 'peine' passage is emphasised by its excessive length. Didi and Gogo agree they will simultaneously finish their sentence, word by word. Their mutual reactions range from astonishment to bewilderment as they gradually reveal the sentence, and discover that they have both uttered exactly the same question: 'Est-ce que c'est la peine.' This conversation was eventually omitted by Beckett, apart from the conclusion 'How time flies when one has fun!'

The manuscript also contains a short coda: whether 'it' is worthwhile or not, they have not told each other what they meant by it. Gogo would like to know what Didi was thinking when he asked the question. Unfortunately, they have both forgotten. The scene is so extremely drawn out that the protagonists eventually forget why they asked the question in the first place. Eventually, they agree that the only conclusion they can draw from their exchange is that their simultaneous utterance was a question.

In the manuscript Beckett filled eight pages to draw attention to this question 'Est-ce que c'est la peine'. The scene's excessive length is part of the same dramatic strategy as the one Adorno describes in [note 2]: a simple question in a normal conversation can become terrifying when isolated from its context. The longer the conversation is drawn out, the more isolated it becomes from what preceded it, thus turning into what according to Albert Camus is the only serious problem in philosophy. Camus opened his essay *Le Mythe de Sisyphe* with the subheading 'Absurdity and Suicide': 'There is but one truly serious philosophical problem and that is suicide. Judging whether life is or is not worth living [*la peine d'être vécue*] amounts to answering the fundamental question of philosophy' (Camus, 2005, 1–2; 2000, 17).

What may have prompted Beckett eventually to omit the eight-page passage on the fundamental question is hard to determine, but by indicating Beckett's distance from existentialism in combination with the reference to Hamlet, Adorno's 'Versuch, das Endspiel zu verstehen' indirectly suggests a plausible motivation. The absurdity in Beckett's work was not to be confused with the revolt it incites in Camus. The overarticulated question 'Est-ce que c'est la peine' could readily create the impression of a neat identification with Camus – 'solution clapped on problem like a snuffer on a candle' (Beckett, 1984, 92) – in a similar way as Adorno's reference to Hamlet could all too easily be interpreted as an invitation to reduce *Endgame* to the line 'to be or not to be'. That was evidently not the gist of Adorno's attempt to understand Beckett's work, his 'Versuch, das Endspiel zu verstehen'.

5.

'Verstehen' is the core of a complex hermeneutic enterprise that had an impressive tradition in the German-speaking world, dating back to Friedrich Schleiermacher. The category of the absurd was the most resistant to interpretation, as Adorno noted in his *Aesthetic Theory*, and yet 'the need for interpretation' of especially works like Beckett's was 'the stigma of their constitutive insufficiency' (*Stigma ihrer konstitutiven Unzulänglichkeit*; Adorno, 2003, 194): Adorno's notes on *Endgame* served as a basis not only for his 'Versuch', but also for his *Aesthetic Theory*. For instance, the content of [note 6] recurs in the context of the following statement: 'Works [of art], especially those of the highest dignity, are waiting to be interpreted' (193). Moreover, they are waiting to be continually re-interpreted. His attempt to understand Beckett's *Endgame* was in its turn followed by new attempts, such as the *Neue Versuche Becketts Endspiel zu verstehen: Sozialwissenschaftliches Interpretieren nach Adorno* (1996), a collection of essays edited by Hans-Dieter König. In the first essay, Gunzelin Schmid Noerr interprets Adorno's image of the 'historico-philosophical sundial' as a metaphor of interpretation (Adorno, 1982, 145): the work of art is a rather immobile construction; the connection between the hand and the background – the moving shadow – is effectuated by the sun – 'that is, by the *historically situated* viewpoint of the receiver or interpreter' (Schmid Noerr, 19; emphasis added).

To situate the interpreter Adorno's viewpoint historically, his notes on *Endgame* may be of help. When he wrote them, the most important exponent of hermeneutics was Martin Heidegger. Hans-Georg Gadamer had only just published his *Wahrheit und*

Methode: Grundzüge einer philosophischen Hermeneutik (1960),
building on Heidegger's hermeneutical phenomenology. Since
man is an interpreting being, Heidegger transfigured hermeneutics
into a philosophy, taking the entirety of human existence as its
object. But Heidegger also applied himself to interpreting works
of literature, such as the poetry of Friedrich Hölderlin. In this
respect, Adorno was critical of Heidegger's hermeneutic approach,
arguing that he idolised the poet without reflecting sufficiently on
the form of the poems. Adorno illustrated his criticism by means
of Hölderlin's poetry, discerning a paratactic tendency, which he
related to Beckett. These Hölderlin interpretations thus constitute
a helpful background to investigate the hermeneutic context of
Adorno's notes towards an understanding of Beckett's *Endgame*.

In [note 6] Adorno mentioned 'The enigmatic and the physiognomy of the objective mind. The situations tell us something – but
what?' The form of this note resembles an important note in
Hölderlin's manuscript of his poem 'Wie wenn am Feiertage...'
This unfinished poem on poetics and the role of the poet opens
with a metaphorical construction, comparing the trees in the first
stanza to the poets ('they') in the second stanza:

> As on a holiday, to see the field
> A countryman goes out, at morning, when
> Out of hot night the cooling flashes had fallen
> For hours on end, and thunder still rumbles afar,
> (...) The grapevine drips, and gleaming
> In tranquil sunlight stand the trees of the grove:
>
> So now in favorable weather they stand (...) (193)

As Axel Gellhaus has pointed out (127), Hölderlin added a note
in the manuscript between these two stanzas, that is, between the
'trees' and 'they' (before he has called them the poets):

> Sie, sie mein ich   Aber wie nenn ich sie
> *They, they are what I have in mind   But what do I call them*
> (Hölderlin, 1989, folio 14b)

The space between 'ich' and 'Aber' is a significant blank, in
the sense of the 'Blanks for when words gone' in *Worstward Ho*

(Beckett, 2009, 99). Not only does it indicate the difficulty of finding the right word, it also intensifies the 'paratactic tendency' Adorno discerns in Hölderlin's poetry, as he explains in his essay 'Parataxis' (Adorno, 1981, 473). In this essay Adorno polemically criticises Heidegger's 'synthesising' interpretation by contrasting it with paratactic features. Heidegger's method disturbed the relationship between content and form, according to Adorno (468–69), and this form was distinctly paratactic. Adorno's concern with parataxis – a characteristic also of notetaking in general – sheds light on his own notes concerning Beckett's work.

In 'Parataxis', he even makes an explicit reference to Beckett (479), via a common point of reference: Beethoven. Again, the identification is not neat, but rather complex and to some extent paratactic itself, in that it 'places side by side' (Gr. *para-tassein*) instead of 'clapping solution on problem'. Adorno first compares literature to music, Hölderlin to Beethoven, and subsequently links both of them to Beckett. '[A]s so often in Beethoven's late style' (473) serial elements offer resistance against harmony. Without having read *Dream of Fair to Middling Women*, Adorno alludes to the same aspect as Belacqua's reference to Beethoven's 'compositions where into the body of the musical statement he incorporates a punctuation of dehiscence' (1992, 139), echoed in Beckett's German letter to Axel Kaun (9 July 1937): 'Is there any reason why that terrible materiality of the word surface should not be capable of being dissolved, like for example the sound surface, torn by enormous pauses, of Beethoven's seventh Symphony (…)?' ('Gibt es irgendeinen Grund, warum jene fürchterlich willkürliche Materialität der Wortfläche nicht aufgelöst werden sollte, wie z.B. die von grossen schwarzen Pausen gefressene Tonfläche in der siebten Symphonie von Beethoven (…)?'; Beckett, 1984, 53; 172). Adorno referred to the same dissolved sound surface of Beethoven's late works to describe the 'paratactic tendency' with which Hölderlin inaugurated a process that – according to Adorno – culminated in 'Beckett's meaningless protocol sentences' (1981, 479).

These protocol sentences [note 11] are the opposite of 'linguistic synthesis' (476), and yet both Hölderlin and Beckett realised that language itself has a synthetic function. The result is linguistic scepticism ('sprachkritische Selbstreflexion'; 476).

6.

In his marginalia to *L'Innommable*, Adorno noted this linguistic scepticism, which he related to Wittgenstein, next to the sentence 'Was geschieht, sind Worte' (Beckett, 2005, 471; 'Ce qui se passe, ce sont des mots', 1998, 98). Whether Beckett was influenced by Wittgenstein at the time he was writing *L'Innommable* is still open to question, and as Shane Weller notes, 'one would surely have to give some weight to Beckett's own claim that he did not read Wittgenstein until the 1950s' (Weller, 228). With reference to Beckett's language, Adorno also observed a 'Difference from Joyce', as he jotted down amongst his notes on *L'Innommable*, in the left margin next to:

> In B[eckett] there is, as a kind of
> counterpoint, something like sound
> common sense. Everything
> so meaningless, yet at the same time the way one
>   speaks
> is so normal, i.e. modern language may have
> shrunken – compared with Kafka's epic language,
>   brought as it were to
> the point of indifference with the absolute
>   subject –
> but [it is] never replaced by <u>linguistic</u> absurdity.
>   (1994, 67)

The note rephrases the same objection against Kafka's style, which from a formal linguistic point of view is still too realistic and does not match the content. That was an aspect Adorno, in contradistinction to Heidegger, also drew attention to with reference to Hölderlin's poetry: the form needs to be taken into account as well. Adorno's idea that in Beckett's case this linguistic form was 'brought as it were to the point of indifference with the absolute subject' reverberates a similar 'zone of indifference' in one of his earlier notes on *Endgame*:

> [note 20] The play takes place in a no man's land, a zone of indifference between inner and outer. What remains of these two in a state of complete alienation.

In his essay, Adorno employs the notion of the 'point' or 'zone of indifference' to indicate how 'pure identity becomes the identity of annihilation, identity of subject and object in the state of complete alienation' (Adorno, 1982, 128). Elsewhere in the essay, this is referred to as 'self-alienation' (138), and in his copy of *L'Innommable* he consequently noted down 'the I as indifference' ('das Ich als Indifferenz'; 1994, 56) next to 'I'm the tympanum, on the one hand the mind, on the other the world, I don't belong to either' (Beckett, 1979, 352).

7.

In the notes on *Endgame*, especially [note 8], Adorno regards this alienation as explicitly linguistic in nature:

> [note 8] There is something absurd in the form of the dialogue itself; meaninglessness of the question-and-answer relationship; gibberish (...) One is alienated from one's own language by B[eckett].* [*(note by Adorno) Situation: One cannot talk any longer. Text p. 22]

The note 'Text p. 22' is a reference to the conclusion of Nagg's story of the tailor, when Hamm shouts 'Silence!' and asks (in the German translation, based on the French version):

> Seid ihr noch nicht am Ende? Kommt ihr nie zu Ende? *(Plötzlich wütend.)* Es nimmt also kein Ende! *(Nagg verschwindet im Mülleimer und klappt den Deckel zu. Nell rührt sich nicht.)* **Worüber können sie denn reden, worüber kann man noch reden?** *(Rasend)* Mein Königreich für einen Müllkipper! (Beckett, 1957, 22; emphasis added)

> Have you not finished? Will you never finish? [*With sudden fury.*] Will this never finish? [*NAGG disappears into his bin, closes the lid behind him. NELL does not move. Frenziedly.*] My kingdom for a nightman! (Beckett, 1990, 103)

The line that is omitted in Beckett's English version could be translated as 'But whereof can they speak, whereof can one still speak?'–which makes it understandable that, especially to German readers like Adorno, this line suggested a proximity to Wittgenstein's *Tractatus Logico-Philosophicus*, notably its last proposition: 'Whereof one cannot speak, thereof one must be silent.'

8.

Whereof did Adorno and Beckett speak when they met? Rolf Tiedemann made an insightful compilation of notes Adorno took after his meetings with Beckett. During their last meeting (in Paris, mid-January 1968) Beckett mentioned the difficulty of writing and called his works 'a desecration of silence' (Tiedemann, 25). He also talked about *Film*, explaining that his text was originally one of three scripts–the other two written by Harold Pinter and Eugène Ionesco–commissioned by Barney Rosset, who 'intended their scripts to form a feature-length trilogy.'

Adorno also met Beckett on 23 September 1967, three days before the première of the *Endspiel* production at the Schiller Theater Berlin under Beckett's direction. According to Adorno's notes, Beckett told him that–as in a chess game–*Endgame* is 'already lost when it starts. After that one simply plays on' (1994, 24). Beckett told Adorno that he had set himself the task of moving in an infinitesimally small room, the problem being how such a movement was possible (24). The way Adorno responded to this description of the closed space texts–'I said: towards the point without dimensions'–already foreshadows *Worstward Ho's* variations on the Shakespearian theme 'The worst is not / So long as one can say, This is the worst' (qtd. in Beckett, 2009, xiii).

The affinity Adorno felt with Beckett was apparently mutual. The next day (Sunday 24 September 1967), Beckett wrote a letter to Barbara Bray, in which he mentions his meeting with Adorno on Saturday afternoon and a few of the topics they talked about–music by Schönberg and Stravinsky, as well as contemporary artists such as the American composer and critic Virgil Thomson. He concluded his account by writing that he did not know why Adorno liked him, nor why he liked Adorno.

9.

Perhaps Beckett's favourite word 'perhaps' is a key to that affinity, in combination with a special attitude to language. 'What is most drastically impoverished in Beckett is language itself', Terry Eagleton wrote in a review of Detlev Claussen's *Theodor Adorno: One Last Genius*: 'Adorno's style reveals a similar austerity as each phrase is forced to work overtime to earn its keep (...) Like Beckett's, Adorno's is a language rammed up against silence, a set of guerrilla raids on the inarticulable' (Eagleton 9–10). The 'inarticulable' may be related to Adorno's most quoted line: 'To write a poem after Auschwitz is barbaric' (Adorno, 1998, 30), and to the sentence that preceded this quotation: 'Even the fullest awareness of the disaster threatens to degenerate into gibberish' (30). This 'gibberish' [note 8] was precisely what Beckett staged, as Adorno notes, resulting in an alienation from one's own language [note 8].

When Adorno mentioned the state of complete alienation in [note 20] he immediately made a link with the concentration camps, as an 'intermediate domain between life and death'. At first sight, the link with Auschwitz may seem far-fetched, but, as Terry Eagleton suggests, it serves as a plausible explanation for the complex affinity between Beckett and Adorno: 'Beckettian humanity is famished, depleted, emptied out of any rich bourgeois inwardness; and though there may be an Irish memory of famine here for Beckett, Adorno could find in this image the poor forked creatures of Auschwitz. The Jew and the Irishman could find common ground in this stark extremity (...). Both understood that one could live and write well only by preserving a secret compact with failure' (Eagleton 9).

10.

Still, Hamm's question remains: 'Worüber können sie denn reden, worüber kann man noch reden?' The German translation was based on the French sentence, omitted in the English version: 'Mais de quoi peuvent-ils parler, de quoi peut-on parler encore? (*Frénétique*) Mon royaume pour un boueux!' (Beckett, 1981, 38).

In this original version of 'My kingdom for a nightman!' the 'boueux' is explicitly related to 'la boue'. Adorno rightly connects this 'mud' both to biblical 'dust' and to filthy 'muck' in [note 28]. In the bilingual (English/German) edition of *Eh Joe*, the line 'Mud thou art' (cf. Beckett, 1990, 365) is translated by Erika and Elmar Tophoven as 'Dreck bist du'. In the copy of this edition, inscribed 'for Rich [Cluchey] affectionately from Sam, Stuttgart Jan. 79', Beckett has added the reference Genesis III 19 in the margin (UoR MS 3626), linking the biblical line directly to the 'Dreck', as Adorno did in [note 28]:

[note 28] Take the theological 'unto dust shalt thou return' literally: filth (*Dreck*), the most intimate, chamber pot, piss, pills are the universal as remainder. Abstractionism and concretism.

The opposition between 'abstractionism and concretism' is elaborated at the beginning of the essay: 'Ontology appeals to those who are weary of philosophical formalism but who yet cling to what is only accessible formally. To such unacknowledged abstraction, Beckett affixes the caustic antithesis by means of acknowledged subtraction' (123–4). The 'Dreck' and the relation to the biblical 'unto dust shalt thou return', on the other hand, is mentioned towards the very end of Adorno's essay (1982, 150).

Whereas, in the essay, these concepts ('Dreck' and the opposition 'abstractionism/concretism') are separated by more than 25 pages, the notes paratactically place them side by side and thus shed some light on the way they were related, from Adorno's point of view: the 'caustic antithesis' (124) between the language of existential ontology à la Heidegger on the one hand and Beckett's language on the other is a matter of abstractionism versus concretism. The problem with existentialist ontology is its 'hieratic language':

[note 27] The hieratic language alone turns the radicalism of existential ontology into a lie. While one confronts nothingness, while everything is being questioned, the bathos of this questioning already warrants the meaning it pretends to know nothing about.

Against this 'hieratic language' Beckett posits his 'regressive language' (*regredierende Sprache*), as Adorno calls it (1982, 119; 1981, 281). And he does so by means of 'subtraction' (123). 'What becomes of the absurd, after the characters of the meaning of existence have been torn down, is no longer a universal – the absurd would then be yet again an idea – but only pathetic details which ridicule conceptuality' (128). Instead of making play with empty abstractions or universals, Beckett subtracts, as the last of Adorno's notes on *L'Innommable* summarises: 'Not abstraction but subtraction'. The same phrase recurs in another notebook with reference to *Godot* (notebook V, 44, in Tiedemann, 1994, 23). The 'remainder' after this subtraction is the only 'universal' that is left: 'filth (*Dreck*), the most intimate, chamber pot, piss, pills are the universal as remainder' [note 28]. If this is the only 'universal' that remains, Beckett's subtraction indeed 'extends ontological abstraction literally *ad absurdum*' (Adorno, 1982, 124) and 'liquidates' the subject 'to the point where it constricts into a "this-here"' (*ein Diesda*; 1982, 124; 1981, 287).

11.

This 'this here' foreshadows 'this this here' in 'what is the word' (Beckett, 2009, 133). The subtracted concreteness in Beckett's writings can be illustrated by means of the 'small heart-shaped plastic pot' at the bedhead of the protagonist in the manuscripts of *Stirrings Still*: 'For improbable as he may be he is not so improbable as not to must needs from time to time relieve himself' (qtd. in Van Hulle, 166). This seemingly 'unbeckettian' realism can be circumscribed by what Adorno calls 'Sachlichkeit' – a term that is usually translated as 'objectivity' because of the Neue Sachlichkeit ('New Objectivity') movement, with artists such as George Grosz, Max Beckmann and Otto Dix. The realistic style of this 1920s movement, which ended with the rise of Nazism, constituted a counterpoint to contemporaneous Abstract art and Expressionism. Against the ecstatic bathos of what Adorno called 'the expressionist "Oh Man"' (*das expressionistische O Mensch*; 1982, 127; 1981, 291) the 'Neue Sachlichkeit' focused on plain objects. In that sense, 'objectivity' also applies to Beckett's 'plastic pot'. But there is an important difference, for Beckett deleted the reference to the concrete chamber pot after the second draft. Hence Adorno's idea of a *hidden* objectivity in [note 31]:

[note 31] Addition re language. (...) Removal of ornaments. In B[eckett], the objectivity is so hidden that – by removing the meaning – it becomes mysterious and starts to fluoresce.

Yet, even though the concrete object is omitted, the remainder is not empty abstractionism; the subtraction somehow leaves its textual remainder: 'In the act of omission, that which is omitted survives through its exclusion' (Adorno, 1982, 125).

12.

The remainder paradoxically creates a 'Tremendous richness of allusions and links', which Adorno relates to 'the malignant joke, she cries ergo she lives' [note 13]. Adorno mixes up the sexes of Nagg and Nell, but the Cartesian parody remains just as malignant and the reference just as rich: 'Clov: Il pleure. – Hamm: Donc il vit.' (Beckett, 1981, 84) The 'ergo' in Beckett's 'lacrimo ergo sum' serves as a marker that signals what Ruby Cohn later called 'cruel logic': 'Beckett introduces a device into *Fin de partie* – what I call cruel logic – that enters the dialogue by a seemingly neutral conjunction "alors" [then]' (229). Adorno had already noticed this device. In his essay he adds another example of the 'malignant joke' by quoting the following passage:

HAMM: Open the window.
CLOV: What for?
HAMM: I want to hear the sea.
CLOV: You wouldn't hear it.
HAMM: Even if you opened the window?
CLOV: No.
HAMM: Then it's not worthwhile opening it?
CLOV: No.
HAMM: (*violently*) Then open it! (qtd. in Adorno, 1982, 141)

Adorno draws attention to the cruel conjunction and even presents it as an interpretative key: 'One could almost see in Hamm's last 'then' the key to the play. Because it is not worthwhile to open the window, since Hamm cannot hear the sea (...) he insists that Clov open it. The nonsense of an act becomes a reason to accomplish it' (Adorno, 1982, 141). Apart from this final 'Then', the preceding one is interesting as well. In the French version, Hamm's reaction after Clov's first 'non' is: 'Alors ce n'est pas la peine de l'ouvrir' (Beckett, 1981, 87). This is the same 'peine' as in the fundamental question Beckett omitted from the *Godot* manuscript. If the answer to Camus's fundamental question whether life is worth living or not would be 'no', the same 'cruel logic' of the dialogue demands the reply: 'Then live it!'

13.

'Yes, life I suppose, there is no other word' (Beckett, 1990, 149). According to Adorno's notes on *L'Innommable*, 'Living is dying because it is a not-being-able-to-die' (1994, 65). He did not find the time to accomplish the last phase in the composition process: the 'writing up' or what he called 'textieren' (Adorno in Tiedemann, 1994, 34). This phase did materialise in the case of his interpretation of *Endgame*. The transition from the paratactic notes to their integration into a structured whole involved shuffling. For instance, he decided to move part of [note 9] to the very end of the essay: 'It is as if consciousness wished to endure the end of its own physical presence, while looking it in the face. Connection with Proust' [note 9]. The final paragraph elaborates on this connection with Proust:

> Proust, about whom the young Beckett wrote an essay, is said to have attempted to keep protocol on his own struggle with death, in notes which were to be integrated into the description of Bergotte's death. *Endgame* carries out this intention like a mandate from a testament. (Adorno, 1982, 150)

The night before Proust died, he was still working. According to Céleste Albaret (421), he dictated some passages to her, notably a description of the doctors gathering around the deathbed of the fictitious writer Bergotte and a reflection regarding the way one is suddenly treated differently as soon as it is clear that one is dying anyway. For instance, all of a sudden one is allowed to drink champagne, which used to be forbidden by the doctors. Consequently, the moribund decide to order the brands from which they had always abstained. There is, Proust concludes, something 'vile' about 'this incredible frivolity of the moribund' (*cette incroyable frivolité des mourants*; Proust, 1989, vol. 3, 1739, note [691]a). The conscious confrontation with one's own end constituted an appropriate closing paragraph for Adorno's essay. It is indicative of the importance Adorno attached to the groping quality of notetaking that, of all his notes on *Endgame*, it was a reference to another author's notes for which he reserved this prominent place.

WORKS CITED

Adorno, Theodor W. (1981), 'Versuch, das Endspiel zu verstehen', *Noten zur Literatur*, Frankfurt am Main: Suhrkamp.

Adorno, Theodor W. (1982), 'Trying to Understand *Endgame*', trans. Michael T. Jones, *New German Critique* 26: *Critical Theory and Modernity* (Spring-Summer 1982), pp. 119–50.

Adorno, Theodor W. (1991), 'Trying to Understand *Endgame*', trans. Shierry Weber Nicholsen, *Notes to Literature*, New York: Columbia University Press, 1991, pp. 241–75.

Adorno, Theodor W. (1998), 'Kulturkritik und Gesellschaft', in *Gesammelte Schriften* 10.1 (Kulturkritik und Gesellschaft I), Darmstadt: Wissenschaftliche Buchgesellschaft, 1998, pp. 11–30.

Adorno, Theodor W., Walter Boehlich, Martin Esslin, Hans-Geert Falkenberg and Ernes Fischer (1994), ' "Optimistisch zu denken ist kriminell": Eine Fernsehdiskussion über Samuel Beckett', *Frankfurter Adorno Blätter III*, ed. Theodor W. Adorno Archiv, Munich: edition text+kritik, pp. 78–122.

Albaret, Céleste (1973), *Monsieur Proust*, ed. Georges Belmont, Paris: Laffont.

Beckett, Samuel (1957), *Endspiel und Alle die da fallen*, trans. Elmar Tophoven, Frankfurt am Main: Suhrkamp.

Beckett, Samuel (1979), *The Beckett Trilogy: Molloy, Malone Dies, The Unnamable*, London: Picador.

Beckett, Samuel (1981), *Fin de partie*, Paris: Éditions de Minuit.

Beckett, Samuel (1984), *Disjecta*, ed. Ruby Cohn, New York: Grove Press.

Beckett, Samuel (1990), *The Complete Dramatic Works*, London: Faber and Faber.

Beckett, Samuel (1993), *Dream of Fair to Middling Women*, New York: Arcade Publishing.

Beckett, Samuel (1995), *The Complete Short Prose 1929–1989*, ed. S. E. Gontarski, New York: Grove Press.

Beckett, Samuel (1996), *En attendant Godot*, Paris: Éditions de Minuit.

Beckett, Samuel (1998), *L'Innommable*, Paris: Éditions de Minuit.

Beckett, Samuel (2005), *Drei Romane: Molloy; Malone stirbt; Der Namenlose*, Frankfurt am Main: Suhrkamp.

Beckett, Samuel (2009), *Company, Ill Seen Ill Said, Worstward Ho, Stirrings Still*, ed. Dirk Van Hulle, London: Faber and Faber.

Camus, Albert (2000), *Le mythe de Sisyphe*, Paris: Gallimard Folio.

Camus, Albert (2005), *The Myth of Sisyphus*, London: Penguin Books.

Claussen, Detlev (2003), *Theodor W. Adorno: Ein letztes Genie*, Frankfurt am Main: S. Fischer Verlag.

Cobley, Evelyn (2005), 'Decentred Totalities in *Doctor Faustus*: Thomas Mann and Theodor W. Adorno', *Modernist Cultures*, Vol. 1, Nr. 2 (Winter 2005), pp. 181–91.

Connor, Steven (2010), 'Beckett and the Loutishness of Learning', *Samuel Beckett Today/Aujourd'hui 22: Debts and Legacies*, ed. Erik Tonning, Matthew Feldman, Matthijs Engelberts, Dirk Van Hulle, Amsterdam: Rodopi, pp. 255–73.

Duckworth, Colin (2007), '*En attendant Godot*: Notes on the Manuscript', *Litteraria Pragensia: Studies in Literature and Culture* 17.33 (July 2007), pp. 31–50.

Eagleton, Terry (2008), 'Determinacy Kills', *London Review of Books* 30.12 (19 June 2008), pp. 9–10.

Gellhaus, Axel (2008), *Schreibengehen: Literatur und Fotografie en passant*, Köln/Weimar/Wien: Böhlau Verlag.

Heidegger, Martin, (1981), *Gesamtausgabe, I. Abteilung: Veröffentlichte Schriften 1910–1976, Band 4: Erläuterungen zu Hölderlins Dichtung*, ed. F.-W. von Herrmann, Frankfurt am Main: Vittorio Klostermann.

Hölderlin, Friedrich (1989), *Sämtliche Werke 'Frankfurter Ausgabe': Historisch-kritische Ausgabe, Supplement II: Stuttgarter Foliobuch*, ed. D. E. Sattler and H. G. Steimer, Frankfurt am Main: Stroemfeld/Roter Stern.

Hölderlin, Friedrich (2001), *Sämtliche Gedichte und Hyperion*, ed. Jochen Schmidt, Franfurt am Main/Leipzig: Insel Verlag.

Hölderlin, Friedrich (2002), *Hyperion and Selected Poems*, ed. Eric L. Santner, New York: The Continuum Publishing Company.

Knowlson, James (1996), *Damned to Fame: The Life of Samuel Beckett*, New York: Simon and Schuster.

König, Hans-Dieter, ed. (1996), *Neue Versuche Becketts Endspiel zu verstehen: Sozialwissenschaftliches Interpretieren nach Adorno*, Frankfurt am Main: Suhrkamp.

Mann, Thomas (1990), *Gesammelte Werke in dreizehn Bänden*, Frankfurt am Main: Fischer Taschenbuch.

Mann, Thomas (1979–95), *Tagebücher*; ed. Peter de Mendelssohn and Inge Jens, Frankfurt am Main: Fischer.

Proust, Marcel (1989), *À la recherche du temps perdu*, 4 vols, ed. Jean-Yves Tadié, Paris: Gallimard Pléiade.

Rosset, Barney (2001), 'On Samuel Beckett's FILM', *Tin House*, Vol. 2, Nr. 2 (Winter 2001). http://www.tinhouse.com/mag/back_issues/archive/issues/issue_6/lostnfound.html

Schmid Noerr, Gunzelin (1996), 'Der Schatten des Widersinns: Adornos "Versuch, das Endspiel zu verstehen" und die metaphysische Trauer', *Neue Versuche Becketts Endspiel zu verstehen: Sozialwissenschaftliches Interpretieren nach Adorno*, ed. Hans-Dieter König, Frankfurt am Main: Suhrkamp, pp. 18–62.

Shakespeare, William (1997), *The Tragedy of Hamlet, Prince of Denmark*, in *The Norton Shakespeare*, ed. Stephen Greenblatt et al., New York and London: Norton, pp. 1668–759.

Tiedemann, Rolf (1994), '"Gegen den Trug der Frage nach dem Sinn": Eine Dokumentation zu Adornos Beckett-Lektüre', *Frankfurter Adorno Blätter III*, ed. Theodor W. Adorno Archiv, Munich: edition text+kritik, pp. 18–77.

Van Hulle, Dirk (2008), *Manuscript Genetics: Joyce's Know-How, Beckett's Nohow*, Gainesville: University Press of Florida.

Voss, Lieselotte (1975), *Die Entstehung von Thomas Manns Roman 'Doktor Faustus', dargestellt anhand von unveröffentlichten Vorarbeiten*, Tübingen: Niemeyer.

Weller, Shane (2009), 'The Art of Indifference: Adorno's Manuscript Notes on *The Unnamable*' in Daniela Guardamagna and Rossana M. Sebellin (eds), *The Tragic Comedy of Samuel Beckett: 'Beckett in Rome', 17–19 April 2008*, Rome: Laterza, pp. 223–37.

GABY HARTEL

Emerging Out of a Silent Void: Some Reverberations of Rudolf Arnheim's Radio Theory in Beckett's Radio Pieces

For Jerry Berndt, the eye that is all ears for Beckett.

As James Knowslon, John Pilling and Mark Nixon have pointed out on many occasions, the young Samuel Beckett went through a distinctly German phase, a 'German fever', in which he felt drawn to the country emotionally and intellectually. Apart from the fact that close relatives and his early love Peggy lived in Kassel, the interest in that part of the world was not surprising in a young man at the time. In the 1920s and 1930s Germany was a conveniently low-budget *Kulturnation*, where intellectuals, bohemians or artists could give their education the finishing touches while at the same time diving into a breathtakingly unrestricted and very affordable metropolitan night-life. Until the

Journal of Beckett Studies 19.2 (2010): 218–227
Edinburgh University Press
DOI: 10.3366/E0309520710000609
© The editors, *Journal of Beckett Studies*
www.eupjournals.com/jobs

election of the National Socialist German Workers' Party (NSDAP) in January 1933, Germany was also one of the most appealing countries for those interested in avantgarde painting, literature, lifestyle, theatre, film and broadcasting. It has been thoroughly documented how much the young wanderer Beckett profited from his extensive travelling, as well as his reading in the artistic fields just mentioned, and I would like to introduce into the discussion a genre which is usually treated only cursorily: Beckett's possible *en passant* reception of early radio theory.

Beckett and radio. This is a complex affair and the topical threads which weave the medium's aesthetics into Beckett's own are too numerous to be tackled in one essay alone. Amongst the many possibilities one aspect strikes me as particulary interesting, and that is the fact that the medium and Beckett's creative endeavours came of age at roughly the same time. Just when the young scholar started to push beyond the restrictions of the received rules of literature and to look for formal inspiration in other media, such as film, painting and music, advanced radio practitioners, writers, composers and intellectuals in Germany were wondering how to use the language of broadcasting in a media-specific way, that is to say more creatively than to have actors read or perform stiffly in front of a microphone. An ambitious symposium on 'Dichtung und Rundfunk' (poetry and broadcasting) was held in Kassel, Germany, in autumn 1929 with, amongst others, Alfred Döblin, Arnold Zweig, Arnolt Bronnen, Hermann Kasack as passionate participants. The transcriptions of what was said during this gathering of writers, journalists, radio practitioners and heads of radio stations, in search of forms of expression in this exciting new medium, correspond strikingly with Beckett's praise for Joyce's poetic language in his first essay *Dante ... Bruno.Vico..Joyce* published that very year. Beckett celebrated the flexibility and sensory density of language in *Work in Progress*, the artistic unity of content and form, and the fact that 'it is not written at all. It is not to be read – or rather it is not only to be read. It is to be looked at and listend to. His writing is not *about* something; it is *that something itself*' (Beckett, 1929, 14). In very much the same tone the more adventurous participants of the Kassel symposium greeted broadcasting as a chance to free writing from the 'restrictions of the letter' and to reintroduce into language a long neglected stylistic openess and materialist versatility, a liveliness and orality.[1] As did the young Beckett, they complained that literature had been written to death and that the warmth, the performative quality, spontaneity and iconicity of earlier literature should now be rediscovered after having been stifled for centuries by the dictatorship of the printing press. Some expressed their satisfaction with the fact that the new technology had finally reinstalled the central position of the oldest medium of transmission, the human voice. There was hope that now that the word had found a new medium of expression, writers would again make use of the aural, vocal and gestural qualities of language.

It is unlikely that Beckett was aware of this cultural debate, even though he visited Kassel four times in 1929, but he would have come across the central ideas expressed here in his later reading as they were quoted or rephrased in the critical debate which accompanied the introduction of sound into film. When, in 1936, Beckett read the texts by film makers and film theoreticians Sergej Eisenstein, Vselvolod Pudovkin and Rudolf Arnheim in order to learn more about film, it would have been very difficult for him to miss their crucial remarks on the artistic use of sound in film, which in the case of Arnheim was demonstrated by his analysis of radio plays in his seminal study *Film als Kunst* (1932; English translation: *Film*, 1933). Judging by Beckett's critical writing at the time, the thoughts voiced by media critic and radio author Rudolf Arnheim (1904–2007) would have been appealing to him. It is, for instance, in Arnheim's *Film* that we find the consiliatory passage about the future of the artistic, two dimensional silent film, which Arnheim envisaged as prospering and coexisting alongside the naturalistic, colour and sound film, and which Beckett referred to nearly verbatim in his letter to Thomas Mac Greevy on 6 February 1936. Arnheim writes a long chapter on radio plays, then more advanced in the artistc use of sound than film, to demonstrate the aesthetic potential of pure sound and 'because it provides a very obvious opportunity for dealing seperately with the acoustic factor of sound film'. He then goes on to explain that in his view, 'silent film and radio play are the father and mother of sound film' (Arnheim, 1933, 215).

Arnheim's writing about the effects of pure sounds would not have met the young scholar's mind unprepared though: Beckett had a highly sensitive ear as we can deduct from his own, very aural writing. Furthermore, in his general reading of the time he would have encountered the phenomenology of hearing: 'Sounds are as close to us as our thoughts' is after all one of George Berkeley's central observations. Another helpful insight into the effect of listening might have come via Friedrich Nietzsche. When Nietzsche's Zarathustra returns to his cave from a longer period of aimless wandering, he is surprised by a multitude of voices which reverberate from the cave's walls, and they impress the approaching walker to such an extent that Nietzsche coins a new word to describe the phenomenon: 'Hörspiel' (audio drama), thereby introducing to cultural history, *avant la lettre*, a standard expression of today's radio art (Nietzsche, qtd. in Meyer, 61).

The uncannily immaterial presence of sounds severed from a traceable source, of disembodied voices reaching the listener from a non-defined, vast space, and the power they excercised on the human mind, permeated nineteenth-century thought. There was talk of voices from the grave and of mysterious messages, emanating from the mesmerising electric field of parallel worlds.[2] These ideas surfaced after the invention and public introduction of telephony, of the phonograph cylinder and the gramophone. In 1878 Edison presented his invention of the phonograph in tune with the *zeitgeist* as a machine, capable of producing acousting deathmasks in that they could record the 'last words of the dying' (in *Scientific American*, qtd. in Hagen, 2001, 23). In the twentieth century, disembodied voices as overpowering master's devices haunted even the purely visual field, as in one of the most arresting scenes in Fritz Lang's silent movie *Dr. Mabuse. Der Spieler* (1922). Here, the overwhelming power of the wicked hypnotist is demonstrated by him speaking to his awe-stricken followers from behind a curtain. When, finally, one of them finds the courage to check who is behind the curtain, it turns out that the voice came from a gramophone record. A year later, when radio waves were first broadcast in Germany from the roof of Berlin's 'Vox-Haus', the event triggered off a heated public debate which mirrored the troubled thoughts of the preceeding century: again there was talk of voices from the grave conquering the unrestricted ether space, of voices as acoustic death-masks of their bearers as well as voice as the earthly fingerprint of man (cf. Hartel and Kaspar).

As one can see, quite a few opinions attributed mystic powers to the new radio medium, and the phrasing was not seldom close to what Beckett referred to as the 'brothers Grimm-machinery' (qtd. in Pilling, 113), thereby ironically hinting at an atmospheric cultural ambience of the country he liked to visit.

That ether, the 'background of a silent void' (*Folie des schweigenden Nichts*), as Rudolf Arnheim defined the essence of radio in 1933, should in the new, 'ideally blind' radio art be inscribed with purely aural traces like voices, sounds, words or their absence, to produce a visceral and totally non-visual effect is an idea that Beckett would have found appealing.

In a letter of 5 July 1956, Beckett wrote to Nancy Cunard that he had 'Never thought about Radio play technique but in the dead of t'other night got a nice gruesome idea full of cartwheels and dragging feet and puffing and panting which may or may not lead to something' (Knowlson, 428). However, reading my way through the history of the German radio avant-garde made me wonder whether, contrary to his own statement, Beckett might not have had a theoretical *hinterland* – if only subconsciously – when starting to work in the medium in 1956. It is a feeling supported by John Morris, then BBC Radio Three controller, who commented on his first meeting with Beckett: 'I got the impression that he has a very sound idea of the problems of writing for radio and that we can expect something pretty good' (Knowlson, 428).

How would Beckett have shaped this 'sound idea'? When stating that he 'never thought about Radio play technique', Beckett may have forgotten what Rudolf Arnheim wrote about radio drama in *Film*. But since, as stated above, this book contains an argument for the artistic superiority of the silent film over the sound film, it is very likely that it was amongst the 'lot of works on cinema' which Beckett borrowed from 'young Montgomery' and which he read in 1936 (letter to MacGreevy, 29 January 1936; Beckett, 2009, 356).[3] It would be interesting to find out whether Beckett's interest in Arnheim might have led him to read the latter's study *Radio* (1936), which appeared in English in a translation by Beckett's acquaintance Herbert Read (together with Margaret Ludwig) the same year.

As can be expected from a trained *gestalt-theorist*, Rudolf Arnheim was interested in the effects that the artistic material of film and radio had on the human mind, and it is for this reason that he set out to define radio from a sensory and material angle. One of his first essential statements on radio art in *Film* is that it should not be considered as theatre for the blind, insofar as it did not appeal to the eye at all – not even to the 'inner eye' –, but rather to the ear alone (Arnheim, 1933, 214). In *Radio* Arnheim dedicates a whole chapter to the 'Praise of Blindness' (1936, 133–204), in which he passionately stresses that one of the elemental gains of radio is precisely the fact that nothing is to be seen. Arnheim is convinced 'that radio drama, in spite of the undeniable feature of an abstract and unearthly character, is capable of creating an entire world complete in itself out of the sensory materials at its disposal. A world of its own which does not seem defective or to need the supplement of something external such as the visual' (Arnheim, 1936, 137–8).

Arnheim's decisive position seems to be echoed in Beckett's strict objection to a staged version of his first radio play *All That Fall*: '*All That Fall* is a specific radio play, or rather radio text, for voices, not bodies. I have alread refused to have it 'staged' and cannot think of it in such terms. [. . .] to 'act' is to kill it. Even the reduced visual dimension it will receive from the simplest and most static of readings [. . .] will be destructive of whatever quality it might have and which depends on the whole thing's coming out of the dark [. . .]' (letter to Barney Rosset, 27 August 1957). Arnheim stresses the time-based quality of the medium by making clear that everything that exists in radio, all action 'grows piecemeal from nothingness' (Arnheim, 1936, 215) through the gradually emerging sounds – be they words, music, or everyday sounds. Within this context he also pleads not to consider language superior to sound and to 'resign[. . .] the word to the sound of the thing itself at the right moment' (140). (Here again, an echo of Beckett's radio oeuvre comes to mind: the scene when Henry in *Embers* expresses his feelings of comfort or discomfort by respectively referring to the clicking together of two large pebbles and to 'this sucking' of the nearby sea). The thought of a time–based art, too, might have sounded appealing to Beckett in the 1930s, since he had stated a few years earlier in his monograph on *Proust*: 'At best, all that is realized in Time, whether in Art or Life, can only be possessed successively by a series of partial annexations and never integrally and at once' (Beckett, 1931, 31).

The art of radio is, for Arnheim, an abstract sensation of time passing, and in this it can give the listener a very unusual physical experience, which only purely acoustic art can produce. He writes enthusiastically about the 'new and thrilling, purely musical experience' of hearing music 'emerging out of the empty void', and goes on to say:

> Time passes most perceptively. Nothing of what has just been is left the next moment: only the course of the single line of melody exists; all the action is pure movement. [...] Whoever has nothing to play vanishes completely out of the picture, simply does not exist. If the piece is *adagio*, then the whole world is *adagio*; if it is *allegro*, then nothing exists but the rushing course of the rapid motion [...] Only in this way does the incessant alteration in the body of sound [...] really penetrate to the senses. (Arnheim, 1936, 145–6)

To me this description of a non-verbal, totally visceral reception of an aural work of art suspended in a 'silent void' displays a tempting parallel to a passage in Beckett's letter to Axel Kaun, in which he, conveniently, employs a musical image to describe his ideal use of language: 'Or is literature alone to be left behind on that old, foul road long ago abandoned by msuic and painting? [...] Is there any reason why that terrifyingly arbitrary materiality of the word surface should not be dissolved, as for example the sound surface of Beethoven's Seventh Symphony is devoured by huge black pauses, so that for pages we cannot perceive it as other than a dizzying path of sounds connecting unfathomable chasms of silence?' (Beckett, 2009, 518–19). And Arnheim's claim that 'whoever has nothing to play [...] simply does not exist' is potentially commented on, self-referentially, by Mrs. Rooney in *All That Fall*: 'Don't mind me. Don't take any notice of me. I do not exist. The fact is well known' (Beckett, 1984, 19).

For Arnheim, the effectiveness of radio art arises from an immediate directness with which it surprises the listener, when different voices, tones or sounds emerge as 'fresh products' from nothingness, at the moment of their reception. Arnheim asks the radio artist to concentrate on the necessary coincidence of content and form, and – as a good modernist – he also stresses the importance of formal economy. Arnheim also, for the first time in radio theory, points out the material quality of voices and talks about them as if they were instruments; he even places the right choice of tonality and expressiveness of voices over the content. The radio artist should not, he warns, value content higher than its presentation, as one might bore the listener to death and fall short of the high artistic potential of the new medium. Arnheim also hypothetically wonders what would happen if one might stage a contest between language and music as a radio play.[4] And in one of the book's illustrations, the photo of a broadcasting studio in Königsberg (now Kaliningrad), he quotes the highly suggestive motto: 'everything sounds, even the void'. As Kurt Weill did in 1925, Arnheim felt strongly about treating language and music on the same level as sound material, and he mentions the artistically advanced, twelve minute long radio play *Weekend* (1930) as an example. This is a work by experimental film maker Walter Ruttmann, who used the new technology of sound film to create a pure sound track of a typical Berlin weekend. Here, language appears only as quotes in the compositional flow of every day sounds. Another of the medium's characteristics Arnheim explores in his introduction to *Radio* is the fact that the listeners' minds can themselves serve as a wireless, in that by switching channels they can create their own, personal programme. This is reminiscent of Beckett's display of Henry's mind in *Embers*: as if it were a radio set it receives its own ghostly voices from memory. The character of Opener, too, in *Cascando*, seems to be the voice of an (abstracted) announcer, who for Arnheim is 'the simplest form, the most original form of broadcast' (Arnheim, 1936, 142). *Cascando*'s Opener switches into the various channels of the creative mind to create a radiophonic presence.

Most of the aspects mentioned – and many more that are described by Arnheim – were put into practice by Beckett, when, from 1956 onward, he embarked on the task of being an artist who, as Arnheim defined the radio author, is 'given the exciting possibility of making an amazing new unity out of pure form and physical reality with the combined help of three means – sound and voice; music; words' (Arnheim, 1936, 15). Beckett may have developed his sensitivity for the needs of the medium solely from his experience as a radio listener. But I like to think that this was not the case and that with his own radio pieces he materialised Arnheim's thoughts on the power of sound emerging from the silent void.

I would like to end with a remark on the cultural influence Beckett may have had as an intermediator of the forgotten radio-avantgarde, before its rediscovery in the late 1980s by radio artist Andreas Ammer and the band *Einstürzende Neubauten* amongst others. Exceptionally advanced as the thoughts on aesthetics, politics and the practice of radio art may have been before 1933 in Germany, they were so brutally and effectively stifled by the National Socialists' cultural politics, that they were completely forgotten after the end of the Second World War. Unlike painting, which went back to its modernist roots after the forced interruption from 1933 to 1945, the fruitful experiments in radio art had to be reinvented in the 1960s by dedicated radio people such as Klaus Schöning and his 'Studio Akustische Kunst' at Westdeutscher Rundfunk, Cologne.

In following his own aesthetic interests in the art of radio, and by remembering his reading of Arnheim, Beckett might, indeed, have brought a forgotten art back to Germany in the late 1950s, without anyone at the time noticing the historical background.

NOTES

1. Stiftung Archiv der Akademie der Künste (ed.), *Dichtung und Rundfunk 1929* (exhibition catalogue), Berlin 2000.

2. Cf. Gaby Hartel and Frank Kaspar, 'Die Welt und das geschlossene Kästchen', in Felderer, 2004, 133ff.

3. Beckett may also have come across Arnheim's articles on sound film in the back numbers of *Close–Up*, since it prided itself, in the words of its editors, of being 'the first magazine (all British) to approach film from the artistic, psychological and educational points of view ... [and it provides] a searchlight on all original and experimental work in every country. Valuable information and comment from famous writers and thinkers throughout the world' (qtd. in Gillespie, 159).

4. Cf. Rudolf Arnheim's 'Wohin geht der Rundfunk?', in Dietrichs, 2004, 214.

WORKS CITED

Arnheim, Rudolf (1933), *Film*, London: Faber and Faber.

Arnheim, Rudolf (1936), *Radio*, London: Faber and Faber.

Beckett, Samuel (1929), 'Dante...Bruno.Vico.Joyce', *transition* 16–17, pp. 242–53.

Beckett, Samuel (1931), *Proust*, London: Chatto & Windus.

Beckett, Samuel (1984), *Collected Shorter Plays of Samuel Beckett*, London: Faber and Faber.

Beckett, Samuel (2009), *The Letters of Samuel Beckett*, Vol. 1: 1929–1940, ed. Martha Dow Fehsenfeld and Lois More Oppenheim, Cambridge: Cambridge University Press.

Dietrichs, Helmut H., ed. (2004), *Rudolf Arnheim, Die Seele in der Silberschicht, Medientheoretische Texte Photographie – Film – Rundfunk*, Frankfurt/M: Suhrkamp Verlag.

Gillespie, Diane F. (1993), *The Multiple Muses of Virginia Woolf*, Columbia: University of Missouri Press.

Hagen, Wolfgang (2005), *Das Radio*, Munich: Wilhelm Fink.

Hagen, Wolfgang (2001), '"Was mit Marconi began"...Radio und Psychoanalyse', *Neue Rundschau*, 112.4), pp. 21–36.

Hartel, Gaby and Frank Kaspar (2004), 'Die Welt und das geschlossene Kästchen', in *Phonorama. Eine Geschichte der Stimme als Medium*, ed. Brigitte Felderer, Berlin: Matthes & Seitz.

Knowlson, James (1996), *Damned to Fame; A Life of Samuel Beckett*, London: Bloomsbury.

Meyer, Petra Maria (1993), *Die Stimme und ihre Schrift. Die Graphophonie der akustischen Kunst*, Vienna: Passagen Verlag.

Pilling, John (2005), 'Beckett and "the German fever": Krise und Identität in den 1930ern', in *Der unbekannte Beckett. Samuel Beckett und die deutsche Kultur*, eds. Therese Fischer-Seidel and Marion Fries-Dieckmann, Frankfurt/M.: Suhrkamp Verlag.

TINE KOCH

Searching for the Blue Flower: Friedrich Schlegel's and Samuel Beckett's 'Unending Pursuits' of 'Infinite Fulfilment'

1. 'Schlegel pfui!' – Beckett and German Romanticism

'Schlegel (pfui!)' ['Schlegel (bah!)']¹ – in Samuel Beckett's extensive reading notes concerning the history of German philosophy and literature, this is the only direct comment one can find about one of the leading representatives of the literary movement of Early Romanticism in Germany: Friedrich Schlegel (TCD MS 10967, 253; qtd. in Tonning, 184). Despite this apparently unambiguous rejection, the frequent references throughout Beckett's works clearly show that Beckett was profoundly interested in the German Romantic period. This essay builds on existing studies to examine the extent to which the literary movement of German Romanticism can be seen as a backdrop for Beckett's own poetics.²

Journal of Beckett Studies 19.2 (2010): 228–244
Edinburgh University Press
DOI: 10.3366/E0309520710000610
© The editors, *Journal of Beckett Studies*
www.eupjournals.com/jobs

This study argues that although a direct influence at present cannot be proved,[3] there are undoubtedly several astounding correspondences between the implicit poetics of Samuel Beckett and the explicit poetic programme of the Early Romantics around Friedrich Schlegel. At the centre of this investigation stands the specific dynamism which is typical for the Early Romantic poetics, namely its 'unending pursuit' of an imaginable, yet by nature inaccessible aim – that same dynamism that since Novalis' *Heinrich von Ofterdingen* has been called the 'search for the blue flower'. In analogy to this cultural and historical background, I will try to characterise Beckett's works as a sustained attempt to pursue a certain desirable, yet inaccessible goal – and in this sense, as a kind of quest for his own 'blue flower'.

For this purpose, I shall first compare and contrast the aims of the Romantic and the Beckettian quest so that the respective characteristics of the two approaches can be ascertained. Then, in a second step, the specific feature of 'endlessness' to be found in both of the quests will be examined. Finally, the results shall be set against the possible backdrop of a 'paradoxical poetics', a concept that appears to be applicable to both Schlegel and Beckett.

2. Searching for the Blue Flower: Friedrich Schlegel's and Samuel Beckett's 'Unending Pursuits' of 'Infinite Fulfilment'

2.1. '…ALL GIVEN' – BECKETT IN SEARCH OF 'ENTIRETY'

The main tendency of the programmatic thinking of the Early Romantics in Germany was the striving for unity, harmony, and 'universality'. In order to respond to the 'clear consciousness of an infinitely full chaos' with a compensatory counterproposal, Friedrich Schlegel formulated the 'progressive Universalpoesie' ['progressive universal poetics'] (Schlegel, 1882, II, 296/220). The claim for universality of this new poetics found its most obvious expression in the utopia of the 'infinite' or 'absolute book'. This was meant to 'contain', as a kind of literary 'comprehensive project', all single texts of the Early Romantics and to unite them organically as a 'book in eternal progress' (Schlegel 1958, II, 265). With this vision in mind, the ambitious young writers planned to counteract, at least in the field of poetry, the generally felt grief over a lost sense of 'entirety'.

Beckett, by contrast, wanted to make just this experience of chaos and decay not only the engine, but specifically also the main subject of his art:

> The confusion is not my invention.... It is all around us and our only chance now is to let it in. The only chance of renovation is to open our eyes and see the mess. It is not a mess you can make sense of. (Driver, 22)

Nonetheless, Beckett's work establishes organised experiments, in which the overwhelming pleasure of a brief totality might possibly be caught. Already in *Murphy*, this idea is clearly illustrated in a short episode: during a lunchbreak, the protagonist Murphy, who from his daily allowance of five biscuits always eats the best one last, the worst one first, suddenly becomes aware 'that these prepossessions reduced to a paltry six the number of ways in which he could make his meal'. If, however, he could succeed in giving up these preoccupations, Murphy would be confronted with a much larger number of options, and then

> the assortment would spring to life before him, dancing the radiant measure of its total permutability, edible in a hundred and twenty ways! Overcome by these perspectives Murphy fell forward on his face on the grass, beside those biscuits. (Beckett, 1957, 96)

Similar experiments of mathematical combinations and compilations of inventory of every conceivable variation can be found on many occasions. These are, in the general development in Beckett's works, initially of a mostly verbal nature. In the late works, though, the experiments are translated more and more into concrete scenic pictures, as for example in the geometrically measured movement sequences in *Quad*, in which possible 'solos', 'duets' and 'trios' are not governed by chance: 'all given' (Beckett, 1986, 451).

In Beckett's texts there can hence be found a hidden longing for totality and entirety. Also, Beckett's never ceasing attempts to go to the limits – and beyond – of the possible bear witness to the, as it were, 'Romantic' aspiration of attaining a sort of universality. The fact that Beckett, for this purpose, first transfers the possible to the level of basic, concrete things and categories and then reduces the possible to an extreme does not constitute a contradiction; rather it is the underlying condition for his writing. Since it is virtually impossible to exhaust the absolute possible, a world has to be found whose circumference and radius are drastically reduced, in which the possible becomes manageable, listable, and any 'exhausting' of the same at least conceivable.

This realisation that factual universality is unattainable was shared by the Early German Romantics, whose longing for totality found its aesthetically most valid expression – paradoxically – just in the artistic form of the 'fragment'. The 'apparent contradiction' of fragmentary 'restriction' and the 'idea of the infinite' (Schlegel, 1958, X, 357) was solved theoretically by Friedrich Schlegel in maintaining an interplay of outer restriction and inner boundlessness: aesthetic perfection could be reached if a work was 'sharply limited everywhere, yet within the boundaries endless and inexhaustible' (II, 215). Hence, already for the Early Romantics, the universal, in its totality, could not be evoked except in an indirect manner: as the positive counterpart of the restricted, unfinished.

Beckett obviously had in mind something similar: only within limited experiments are entirety and totality at all conceivable and representable – even if they probably remain out of reach. Yet the simple idea of an experience of that 'fullness' is – as demonstrated by Murphy – absolutely and inexpressibly overwhelming.

2.2. 'GRACE TO BREATHE THAT VOID' – BECKETT IN SEARCH OF 'INFINITY'

In one of the rare comments on his own work, Beckett named two other important aspects which give some information about what he himself was trying to achieve in his literary activity: 'If I were in the unenviable position of having to study my work, my points of departure would be the "*Naught is more real ... [than nothing]*" and the "*Ubi nihil vales ... [ibi nihil velis]*" both already in *Murphy* and neither very rational' (Kennedy, 300).

If one keeps in mind the fascination with this 'nothing', which Beckett had borrowed from Democritus, it follows that Beckett chose with his art a direction which appears to be, at first sight, quite the opposite of the Romantic motto of progression, namely a sort of constant regression, or, in other words, a progressive reduction. As he stated in a late interview: 'I realised that my own way was in impoverishment, in lack of knowledge and in taking away, in substracting rather than in adding' (Knowlson, 352). Indeed, with increasingly simple and economical means, less and less external action and fewer and fewer words, Beckett developed his literary works to a virtual crystallisation art, an 'aesthetics of lessness' (Van Hulle, 286), 'struggling', in Beckett's own words, 'to struggle on... with the next next to nothing' (letter to A. J. Leventhal, 3 February 1959; qtd. in Knowlson, 461). The prime example here is *Breath*, a play not only without words, but also without players, which unfolds before us and passes, literally, in one single breath.

Additionally, in Beckett's late works the drama shifted more and more to the inner stage of consciousness, the 'madhouse of the skull' (Beckett, 1982, 20). Beckett had expressed this retreat in the depths of mind already in *Murphy*:

> Murphy's mind pictured itself as a large hollow sphere, hermetically closed to the universe without. This was not an impoverishment, for it excluded nothing that it did not itself contain. Nothing ever had been, was or would be in the universe outside it but was already present... in the universe inside it. (Beckett, 1957, 107)

If one compares the following Early Romantic fragment with this description, it becomes evident, in view of the astonishing resemblance of both concepts of the human mind as a 'macrocosm', that what Beckett had formulated was not very far away from what had already been expressed by Novalis with regard to the quest for the blue flower:

> We dream of travelling through the universe: yet is the universe not but in ourselves? We do not know the depths of our mind. – The path leads inwards, full of secrets. In ourselves, or nowhere, is eternity with its worlds, are past and future. The outside world is the shadow world, it throws its shadow in the empire of light. (Novalis, 1981, 417)

Therefore, what Beckett aimed at with his 'regressive minimum poetics' seems to be exactly the opposite of what the Early Romantics raised as their ideals. The Romantic longing for boundlessness and fullness, repeatedly called by Schlegel the 'longing for infinity' (Schlegel, 1958, XII, 7–8 and XXIII, 24/52), is obviously opposed to Beckett's longing for nothingness and the greatest possible reduction. However, once again, this opposition turns out to be only on the surface.

As can be demonstrated with almost all of Beckett's charac-ters – for whom the pursuit of nothingness is as typical as for their author – the 'Nothing' is always explicitly positively connoted, as for example in *Murphy*:

> Murphy began to see nothing, that colourness which is such a rare postnatal treat . . . . His other senses also found themselves at peace, an unexpected pleasure. Not the numb peace of their own suspension, but the positive peace that comes when the somethings give way, or perhaps simply add up, to the Nothing, than which in the guffaw of the Abderite naught is more real. (Beckett, 1957, 246)

Furthermore, in the first completed play *Eleuthéria*, the protagonist Victor Krap reports, in a kind of confession, his desperate efforts to separate himself from himself, 'by *being* as less as possible':

> By not moving, not thinking, not dreaming, not speaking, not listening, not seeing, not knowing, not wanting, not being able, and so on. I thought that it was just this my imprisonment. (Beckett, 1995b, 148)

Yet 'Eleutheria' itself is of course the Greek word for freedom. Peace, happiness, freedom: in view of these emphatically positive associations with which the Nothing, the no-more-being and no-more-wanting were invested by Beckett, it becomes quite clear that Beckett's 'nihilism', on closer inspection, can be seen, paradoxically, almost as a continuation of the Romantic striving for boundlessness and infinity, since the Romantic concept can be described in exactly the same terms.

It thus seems that just as universality was conceivable for Beckett paradoxically only within extreme restriction, so was infinity only to be found – if at all – in the 'accidentless One-and-Only, conveniently called Nothing' (Beckett, 1957, 246).

2.3. 'TILL AT LAST HALT FOR GOOD' – BECKETT IN SEARCH OF A 'FINAL REST'

The maxim of 'no-more-wanting' in particular points to the second lodestar of Beckett's works, the above-mentioned 'Ubi nihil vales ibi nihil velis' (cf. Beckett, 1957, 178), which Beckett borrowed from Arnold Geulincx. In the context of an 'absurd' universe, where man is worth nothing and condemned to ceaseless privation and suffering, one of the highest aims of all longing and striving – even more so for such a passionate Schopenhauerian like Beckett – could not be anything but the 'nihil velis', the 'no-more-wanting'. And indeed, the ascetic negation of any wish, 'the will-lessness... in its absolute freedom' (111), can be found as a universal motif at the centre of his work. Hence the Beckettian arcadia is consistently called *neither.*

The famous poem which Beckett handed to the composer Morton Feldman as the 'quintessence' of his work describes the typical climate which can be found in most of his texts: of being constantly on one's way, of searching and to a certain degree also of wanting, which, in a similar manner, had been evoked by the Early German Romantics in many of their novels by means of the literary motif of 'journey' or 'quest' (once again the search for the 'blue flower'). In Beckett's works, though, this wanting is paradoxical, an unceasing, restless 'to and fro in shadow' (Beckett, 1995a, 258), as can be seen over and over again in the predicament of his exhausted characters. In *Rockaby*, for instance, this paradoxical striving almost forms the leitmotif of the play: visually underlined by the to and fro movement of the rocking chair, W's passionate 'More!' stands against the – no less passionate – 'time she stopped' (Beckett, 1986, 435 *et passim*).

Yet at the end of *neither*, something happens that is completely unusual for Beckett: the 'pendulum' finally stands still and finds 'halt for good', and more than that: in coming to a halt, suddenly, a conceivable though 'unspeakable home' on which a 'light unfading' shines, and with it redemption, is found at last. In other words, exhaustion leads to fulfilment.

From this perspective, the rapt admiration of the peace of night, which Beckett had borrowed from the Early German Romantics, also ties in perfectly with the structure of his implicit poetics: 'night and dreams' for the Romantics as much as for Beckett represented a longed-for sanctuary, or even the idea of highest happiness. 'There is nothing higher in human existence than the state of unconsciousness; then one is happy, then one can say that one is content', according to Ludwig Tieck in *William Lovell* (Tieck, 558). We also find this in Beckett, for example in *Eleuthéria*, where the idea appears as follows: being asked by his father when he feels the most happy, little Michel replies *'upon reflection*: I love being in bed, before I fall asleep' (Beckett, 1995b, 114).

Besides Tieck, it was especially Novalis with his *Hymnen an die Nacht* ['Hymns to the Night'] who intensely celebrated the coming of the night which brought with it the beatific redemption of sleep, as for example in the following lines:

> Do you too have a human heart, o dark power?... You only seem to be terryfying–Delicious balm pours from your hand.... [You] give us pleasures, dark and inexpressible, secretly as you are secret yourself, pleasures that gives us the idea of heaven. How poor and childish seems to me the light, with all its colourful things, how pleasant and blessed the day's farewell. (Robertson, 380)

This hymn by Novalis may well have been familiar to Beckett, as it is printed in the original in J. G. Robertson's *History of German Literature*, a book that Beckett studied closely. In any case, it is but a small step from here to Beckett's last television play *Nacht und Träume*. Undoubtedly, Beckett had borrowed its title, its musical recordings and its quite unambiguously 'Romantic' quality directly from Franz Schubert (Schubert op. 43 no. 2 D 827). However, the deeply symbolic motif of the cup passed to the dreamer in his dream might lead us to speculate about an exceptionally direct influence of Novalis on Beckett: 'Delicious balm pours from your hand'.

Furthermore, the tendency of Beckett's characters and voices to incessantly yearn for the end of all things in the most ardent manner, even if, at the same time, they very much fear it, appears, from this perspective, as an absolutely logical consequence. Obviously, the simple prospect of the end, of pausing and stopping, of darkness, silence and stillness is a kind of release, and a blissful one at that. To actually experience this would mean, as Beckett underlines once more in *Ill Seen Ill Said*, a kind of arrival: 'But black. Void. Nothing else. Contemplate that. Not another word. Home at last' (Beckett, 1982, 31).

2.4. 'KNOW HAPPINESS' – BECKETT'S VAIN SEARCHING FOR THE BLUE FLOWER

In his first published story, *Assumption*, Beckett wrote: 'He hungered to be irretrievably engulfed in the light of eternity, one with the birdless cloudless colourless skies, in infinite fulfilment' (Beckett, 1995a, 6). It is noteworthy that this longing for boundlessness, or even 'infinity', is connected here explicitly with the famous blue flower of German Romanticism. One night, the protagonist for the first time sets eyes on the blue flower (precisely like Novalis' Heinrich von Ofterdingen) – and he experiences this as a state of inspiring fulfilment: 'Until at last, for the first time, . . . he was released, achieved, the blue flower, Vega, GOD' (ibid.). The subsequent accumulation of the motif in Beckett's early literary works proves that it is more than just a cunning game for Beckett to cite this Early Romantic *topos* in his first prose piece.

The search for the legendary blue flower had become, thanks to Novalis' *Heinrich von Ofterdingen*, the core concept of Early Romantic poetics. One of the essential characteristics of this quest was that its aim remained unattainable, located in a distance so remote that it could only be imagined. As Friedrich Schlegel stated in one of his philosophical lectures: 'The longing for infinity has to remain longing for good. [...] The visual sense cannot reveal [the Ideal]. The Ideal can never be perceived. The Ideal is generated by speculation' (Schlegel, 1958, XII, 8). Or, on another occasion: 'The absolute highest aim can never be fully reached' (I, 255). The poetic project of the Early Romantics, accordingly, could only be described as an *'endlose Annäherung'* ['unending pursuit'] of the inaccessible as the 'greatest possible effort that the striving force is capable of' (255). For the *progressive Universalpoesie* this had the following consequence: 'Other poetries are complete, and can now be totally analysed. The Romantic poetry is still at the point of being born; indeed it is in its very essence that it can only develop forever, but can never be complete' (Schlegel, 1882, II, 220).

In parallel with Schlegel's dictum, Beckett's universe does not allow for the complete attainment of that which has been desired. Completion is either postponed indefinitely, and will come, like Godot, 'surely tomorrow', or else must coincide with some sort of rest, as we have seen in *neither*. In his late plays, Beckett becomes even more explicit. At the end of *Footfalls*, before the blackout, the stage remains empty for ten seconds; May, who had been going to and fro during the whole play, has disappeared. At the end of *Rockaby*, the rocking chair comes to a stop and W's head sinks down with eyes closed. In thereby connecting the pendulum movement with human existence itself, the stopping and ceasing to be (there) become more or less synonymous, and it seems reasonable to suppose that the desired ideal state, the 'unspeakable home', can possibly never be reached except in death.

It thus seems that in exact parallel to the poetics of Early German Romanticism, the bliss symbolised by the blue flower remained for Beckett throughout his life the highest, yet inaccessible aim of all striving. The perfect 'will-lessness in its absolute freedom' always stayed an illusionary ideal which, to speak once again with Friedrich Schlegel, as it defied perception, could only be 'generated by speculation'. Just as the exhausting of all possibilities can probably only ever be a conceived idea, so the state of longing-lessness, the arcadia of rest and fulfilment that Beckett formulated in *neither*, remains a place of the imagination, but not of actual experience. As the last line of *Ill Seen Ill Said* reveals, 'Know happiness' (Beckett, 1982, 59). It is characteristic of Beckett's unique art that he is able to let resonate, even in the most promising statement, phonetically, its own negation.

The fact that Beckett, in his work, constantly expressed an almost 'infinite' longing for that 'happiness', represents a central, if not *the* central paradox of his creative activity: longing for longing-lessness. Or, as it says in *Worstward Ho*: 'Longing that all go .... Longing go. Vain longing that vain longing go' (Beckett, 1983b, 36). However, it is exactly this paradoxical attitude which opened up Beckett's work – whether he wanted to or not – in spirit to the poetics of the Early German Romantics. Even if the concept of 'will negation' was totally strange to the Romantic tradition[4] – in exactly this vain insatiable longing for the 'nihil velis', Beckett appears as a sort of Romantic, who strove with his art to find the blue flower and the redemption and fulfilment it promised. However, he is a Romantic who at the same time was persuaded – and here we have the cuckoo's egg in Beckett's Romantic breeding ground – that the blue flower could only be found if one could actually stop searching for it – and come to a halt for good on 'that unheeded neither': 'when you cease to seek you start to find' (Beckett, 1963, 43).[5]

3. 'Unending ending or beginning light' – Beckett's Being on 'The Way'

We have seen so far that wherever Beckett negates, reduces, falls silent, this does not happen with the comfort of a cynical nihilism. But this is his way of pursuing his own blue flower, in keeping with his implicit poetics. As for the Early Romantics, this pursuit was 'unending' by nature, and therefore damned to fail.

Yet, despite the acknowledged futility, or even impossibility, of going on, Beckett never quite gave up on his literary quest; as he told Charles Juliet: 'The writing drove me to silence. However, I have to go on... I am facing a cliff and I have to move forward. That's impossible, isn't it? Nevertheless, one can move on. Win some paltry millimetres...' (Juliet, 18). This, once again, shows Beckett in complete accordance with the Early Romantic aesthetics. Based on the realisation that 'all the highest truths... can actually never be completely expressed' (Schlegel, 1882, II, 389), Friedrich Schlegel had postulated the paradox of the 'impossibility of and necessity for complete expression' (Schlegel, 1882, I, 198). Seen against this backdrop, does Beckett's famous statement that 'there is nothing to express, nothing with which to express,... no power to express,... together with the obligation to express' (Beckett, 1983a, 139) not seem almost like a quotation of just that paradox?

Furthermore, the aesthetic consequence seen within the Romantic *Transzendentalpoesie* ['transcendental poetry'], namely the 'continual change of self-creation and self-destruction' by means of self-reflection (Schlegel, 1882, II, 211), appears to be an astoundingly prescient description of Beckett's own 'paradoxical' literary method. Accordingly, at the age of 30, during his trip through Germany, the young author wrote in his diary:

> How absurd, the struggle to learn to be silent in another language!... The struggle to be master of another silence! Like a deaf man investing his substance in Schalplatte [sic], or a blind man with a Leica. ('German Diaries', entry for 18 October 1936; qtd. in Quadflieg, 55)

At first sight, the wish to learn to be silent by means of talking (and writing), or to even become 'master of silence', had something absurd about it, especially for an author. Seen in the Early Romantic tradition, though, this kind of 'transcendental' creative activity would be just the adequate path to follow in order to advance the above-mentioned 'book in progress'.

As his repeated visualisations of dynamic stasis exemplify, Beckett saw no escape from the searching movement anyway – even if it turned out to be an endless loop. A late text from 1981, with the provisional title 'The Way' (later headed '∞'), a kind of 'distillation of all the journeys made by all of Beckett's eternal wanderers' (Lake, 174), can likewise be seen as a kind of condensation of the central theses advocated in this study. In this short text Beckett describes a way which runs in the shape of a horizontal eight:

> Forth and back across a barren same winding one-way way. Low in the west or east the sun standstill. As if the earth at rest. Long shadows before and after. Same pace and countless time. Same ignorance of how far. Same leisure once at either end to pause or not. At either groundless end. Before back forth or back. Through emptiness the beaten ways as fixed as if enclosed. Were the eye to look unending void. In unending ending or beginning light. Bedrock underfoot. So no sign of remains a sign that none before. No one ever before so – (Beckett, 2009, 125 et seq.)[6]

The described way in its aim- and endlessness, already inscribed by the mathematical infinity sign of the horizontal eight, may admittedly demonstrate the futility of any Romantic forward striving, as along such a way 'progress' can never mean to 'get on' in its true sense, and 'forwards' and 'backwards' become interchangeable depending on one's perspective. Yet there are two positive aspects here; on the one hand, there is the deep longing for infinity: 'Were the eye to look unending void'. On the other hand, a 'beginning light'! And this beginning light accompanies the 'unending ending'! Is this the 'light unfading' which will appear one day on 'that unheeded neither'? We cannot be sure, but we may possibly be justified in assuming it.

Finally, one last observation can be made in this connection; in Beckett's notes to *Quad II* we find the following: 'No colour, all four in identical white gowns, no percussion, footsteps only sound, slow tempo' (Beckett, 1986, 454). The passage, 'footsteps only sound' reads (by chance?) just exactly like the line in *neither* which is followed directly by the words 'till at last halt for good'. So we might possibly say that this state represents the preliminary stage to the final stasis Beckett so intensely longed for. Was Beckett himself aware of how close he had already come to his blue flower, with this late pantomime?

In any case, it should be noted, finally, that Beckett too had searched in an, as it were, 'unending pursuit' all his life for his personal blue flower – and that the latter, on closer inspection, – despite the 'Schlegel (pfui!)' verdict – proves to be not at all unlike that of Early German Romanticism. In spite of obvious differences at the level of 'phenomena' (infinity vs infinite void, universality vs nothingness), astoundingly similar concerns can be discovered on both sides at the level of 'ideas': the aspiration to explore the borders between chaos and entirety, resignation and progression, as well as the insatiable striving for boundlessness, redemption and fulfilment.

Despite prevailing differences, the socio-historical starting point for Beckett's literary activity can be compared, too, to that of the Early German Romantics: a present experienced as unsatisfactory and the recent experience of war meant that in both cases power-lessness and chaos constituted the determining experiences of the young authors. In both cases the Socratic motif of ignorance plays a central role in formulating their poetics. As Schlegel wrote: 'While knowledge increases, ignorance increases to the same degree, or rather the knowledge of the ignorance' (Schlegel, 1882, II, 247).

Accordingly, within his own 'poetics of ignorance' (Van Hulle, 2007, 291), Beckett, as a self-appointed 'non-knower', formulated a task for the artist which the Romantics could have endorsed as well: 'To find a form that accommodates the mess' (Driver, 23).

The two approaches, Beckettian and Romantic, have so far been treated as progression versus regression, and thus as by nature contradictory. But on closer inspection they turn out to be not as fundamentally different as at first sight. Of course, all of Beckett's works show episodes of an infinite decline, spirals which screw themselves slowly downwards. However, this Beckettian process of descent might all the same be a sort of ascension – an attempt, 'to go on a trip around the world', to speak with Heinrich von Kleist (whom Beckett admired)[7], to see whether the bolted gates of paradise might be 'accessible somewhere from the back' (Kleist, 559).

As 'The Way' shows, 'forwards' – under certain conditions – can also mean 'backwards', and an 'unending ending' can be a 'beginning light'. Moreover, this 'light', which unexpectedly appears on 'that unheeded neither', is – from a purely geometrical point of view – the event of a transcendency: a revelation from above. Finally, if one takes Beckett literally at his word with regard to his poem *neither*, the following last area of agreement seems to show that the German Romantics and Beckett, fundamentally, appear to be completely in unison: as we have seen, Beckett, when asked for the quintessence of his work, called his very own arcadia towards which he directed all his searching and striving, 'unspeakable home'. When Heinrich von Ofterdingen, the eponymous hero of Novalis' novel, which generated the quest for the blue flower as the symbol of Early German Romanticism *par excellence*, is asked, in the second part of the novel (remarkably entitled *The Fulfilment*) by a passer-by where his travels are actually leading him, he answers straight out: 'Always home' (Novalis, 2007, 163).

I would like to thank my professors Jörg Schönert and especially Barbara Müller-Wesemann for their unfailing encouragement and assistance during the completion of this paper. Moreover, I am very grateful to Nina Stedman for her great help in translating it into English, and to Christian Egners for translating the notes. Finally, I would like to thank Mark Nixon for his valuable support.

NOTES

1. All translations from primary sources into English are mine – except for Beckett's own translations of his works.

2. The current research situation is outlined in Van Hulle and Nixon, 2007, 9 and Ackerley, 2005, 97. Erik Tonning's recent study touches upon the outlined problems in a broader sense, trying to prove exemplary reminiscences of Romantic *Sehnsucht* on the part of the Beckettian characters (cf. Tonning, 2007, 180 et seq.). Further investigations are Nixon (2006), Van Hulle (2006), Ackerley (2005), Laubach-Kiani (2004), as well as contributions in *Samuel Beckett Today/Aujourd'hui* 18: ' "All Sturm and no Drang". Beckett and Romanticism' (2007), ed. D. Van Hulle and M. Nixon. In my doctoral thesis I will try to pursue the possible connections between the Romantic *Transzendentalpoesie* ['transcendetal poetry'] and Beckett's so-called 'metafiction'.

3. I am grateful to Mark Nixon for informing me that there is currently no evidence that Beckett read any literary work of the Early German Romanticism period in the original; the wealth of allusions to and fragments from Romantic writers is apparently taken, as so often with Beckett, from secondary rather than primary sources.

4. The fact that the concept of an ascetic 'negation of the will' was entirely foreign to the Romantic thinkers may have been the decisive reason why we read in Beckett's notes about Friedrich Schlegel 'Schlegel (pfui!)', while on the contrary, in the same sentence, Schopenhauer is called 'dear Arthur'.

5. We can assume that Beckett, with this formulation, also intended to set up an opposite pole to the biblical, 'Seek, and ye shall find' (Matthew 7:7).

6. In an earlier version of the text Beckett makes himself even clearer: 'Briefly once at the extremes *the will set free*' (Beckett, 2009, 125; my italics).

7. Beckett's enthusiasm for Heinrich von Kleist's *Über das Marionetten-theater* is well documented in Knowlson and Pilling, 1979, 275 et seq.

WORKS CITED

A. PRIMARY WORKS

Beckett, Samuel (1957), *Murphy*, New York: Grove Press.
Beckett, Samuel (1963), *Watt*, London: Calder and Boyars.
Beckett, Samuel (1982), *Ill Seen Ill Said*, London: Calder.

Beckett, Samuel (1983a), 'Three Dialogues', in S. Beckett, *Disjecta. Miscellaneous Writings and a Dramatic Fragment*, ed. with a foreword by R. Cohn, London: Calder, pp. 138–45.

Beckett, Samuel (1983b), *Worstward Ho*, London: Calder.

Beckett, Samuel (1986), *The Complete Dramatic Works*, London: Faber and Faber.

Beckett, Samuel (1995a), *The Complete Short Prose 1929–1989*, ed. and with an introduction and notes by S. E. Gontarski, New York: Grove Press.

Beckett, Samuel (1995b), *Eleuthéria*, Paris: Editions de Minuit.

Beckett, Samuel (2009), 'The Way', in S. Beckett, *Company. Ill Seen Ill Said. Worstward Ho. Stirrings Still*, ed. D. Van Hulle, London: Faber and Faber.

Kleist, Heinrich von (1990), 'Über das Marionettentheater', in H. v. Kleist, *Sämtliche Werke und Briefe in vier Bänden*, ed. K. Müller-Salget, Frankfurt/M.: Dt. Klassiker-Verlag, vol. III: *Erzählungen. Anekdoten. Gedichte. Schriften*, pp. 555–63.

Novalis (1981), *Schriften*, ed. R. Samuel in Zusammenarbeit mit H.-J. Mähl u. G. Schulz, Stuttgart/Berlin/Köln/Mainz: Kohlhammer, vol. 2: *Das philosophische Werk I*.

Novalis (2007), *Heinrich von Ofterdingen*, mit einem Kommentar von Andrea Neuhaus. Frankfurt/M.: Suhrkamp.

Schlegel, Friedrich (1958 et seqq.), *Kritische Friedrich-Schlegel-Ausgabe in 35 Bänden*, ed. E. Behler unter Mitwirkung von J.-J. Anstett u. H. Eichner, München/Paderborn/Wien: Schöningh.

Schlegel, Friedrich (1882), *Seine prosaischen Jugendschriften in zwei Bänden*, ed. J. Minor, Wien: Konegen.

Tieck, Ludwig (1999), *William Lovell*, ed. W. Münz, Stuttgart: Philipp Reclam jun.

B. SECONDARY WORKS

Ackerley, Chris (2005), 'Inorganic Form: Samuel Beckett's Nature', *AUMLA: Journal of the Australasian Universities Language and Literature Association*, 104, pp. 79–102.

Ackerley, Chris (2007), 'Samuel Beckett and Anthropomorphic Insolence', in *Samuel Beckett Today/Aujourd'hui 18*, 'All Sturm and no Drang'. Beckett and Romanticism. Beckett at Reading 2006, ed. D. Van Hulle and M. Nixon, Amsterdam/New York: Rodopi, pp. 77–90.

Driver, Tom F. (1961), 'Beckett by the Madeleine', *Columbia University Forum*, 4:3, pp. 21–5.

Juliet, Charles (1986), *Rencontre avec Samuel Beckett*. Saint-Clément-la Rivière: Fata Morgana.

Kennedy, Sighle (1971), *Murphy's Bed: A Study of Real Sources and Sur-Real Associations in Samuel Beckett's First Novel*, Lewisburg: Bucknell University Press.

Knowlson, James and John Pilling (1979), *Frescoes of the Skull. The Later Prose and Drama of Samuel Beckett*, London: Calder.

Knowlson, James (1996), *Damned to Fame. The Life of Samuel Beckett*, London: Bloomsbury.

Lake, Carlton, ed. (1984), *No Symbols Where None Intended. A Catalogue of Books, Manuscripts, and Other Material Relating to Samuel Beckett in the Collections of the Humanities Research Center*, Austin, TX.

Laubach-Kiani, Philip (2004), ' "I Close My Eyes and Try and Imagine Them": Romantic Discourse Formations in *Krapp's Last Tape*', *Journal of Beckett Studies*, 13:2, pp. 125–36.

McMillan, Dougald and Martha Fehsenfeld (1988), *Beckett in the Theatre. The Author as practical Playwright and Director. Volume I: From Waiting for Godot to Krapp's Last Tape*, London: Calder.

Nixon, Mark (2006), ' "Scraps of German": Samuel Beckett reading German Literature', in *Samuel Beckett Today/Aujourd'hui* 16, Notes diverse holo. Catalogues of Beckett's reading notes and other manuscripts at Trinity College Dublin, with supporting essays, ed. M. Engelberts and E. Frost, Amsterdam/New York: Rodopi, pp. 259–82.

Nixon, Mark (2007), 'Beckett and Romanticism in the 1930s', in *Samuel Beckett Today/Aujourd'hui* 18, 'All Sturm and no Drang'. Beckett and Romanticism. Beckett at Reading 2006, ed. D. Van Hulle and M. Nixon, Amsterdam/New York: Rodopi, pp. 61–76.

Quadflieg, Roswitha (2006), *Beckett was here. Hamburg im Tagebuch Samuel Becketts von 1936*, Hamburg: Hoffmann und Campe.

Tonning, Erik (2007), *Samuel Beckett's Abstract Drama. Works for Stage and Screen 1962–1985*, Oxford: Peter Lang.

Van Hulle, Dirk (2006), 'Samuel Beckett's *Faust* Notes', in *Samuel Beckett Today/Aujourd'hui* 16, Notes diverse holo. Catalogues of Beckett's reading notes and other manuscripts at Trinity College Dublin, with supporting essays, ed. M. Engelberts and E. Frost, Amsterdam/New York: Rodopi, pp. 283–97.

Van Hulle, Dirk (2007), ' "Accursed Creator": Beckett, Romanticism and "the Modern Prometheus" ', in *Samuel Beckett Today/Ajourd'hui* 18, 'All Sturm and no Drang'. Beckett and Romanticism. Beckett at Reading 2006, ed. D. Van Hulle and M. Nixon, Amsterdam/New York: Rodopi, pp. 15–29.

MARK NIXON

Chronology of Beckett's Journey to Germany 1936–1937[1] (based on the German Diaries)

28 September 1936

Travels from Dublin to Cobh via Cork, where he visits the grave of Father Prout.

29 September to 2 October 1936

On *S.S. Washington* to Hamburg, with stop at Le Havre. Reading Céline's *Mort à Crédit*.

2 October 1936

After arriving in **Hamburg** he looks at the two Alster lakes, the Reeperbahn and the Landungsbrücke.

3–4 October 1936

Visits various lodgings and decides to move into the Pension of Otto Lembke. Explores Altstadt (old part of town).

5 October 1936

Hears that *Murphy* has been turned down by Simon & Schuster (New York).

Journal of Beckett Studies 19.2 (2010): 245–272
Edinburgh University Press
DOI: 10.3366/E0309520710000622
© The editors, *Journal of Beckett Studies*
www.eupjournals.com/jobs

6 October 1936
First visit to Kunsthalle; looks forward to inspecting Dutch collection. In Deutschlandhaus listens to radio broadcasts by Hitler and Goebbels at the opening of the Winterhilfswerk in Berlin. Notes that war is inevitable.

7 October 1936
Moves to the more comfortable Pension Hoppe. In Altona views Klopstock's grave in grounds of Christiankirche.

8 October 1936
In Kunsthalle, Dutch and modern German painting; admires in particular Jan Josephsz van Goyen and Franz Marc's *Mandrill*. Walks around Binnen– and Außenalster lakes.

9 October 1936
Visits churches: Michaeliskirche, Nikolaikirche and Katharinenkirche. Buys Baedeker *Deutsches Reich*.

10–11 October 1936
Sightseeing –botanical gardens, Elbberg, Reeperbahn. Attends a charity concert for Germans in Spain in Ufa–Palast, hears speech from SS–Gruppenführer Werner Lorenz and sees extracts from anti-soviet documentary film.

12–14 October 1936
In further visits to the Kunsthalle concentrates on Dutch and Flemish landscapes. In Akademische Auslandsstelle, which supports foreign academics, seeks to establish contact to German conversation partners.

15–16 October 1936
Studies German grammar. Visits Jakobikirche, Mohlenhof, Meßberg, Nikolaikirche and other places of interest. Mary Manning Howe writes that Houghton Mifflin interested in *Murphy*.

17 October 1936
Meets Claudia Asher through the Akademische Auslandsstelle, who offers to help Beckett with his German language knowledge. After dinner, fellow lodger Martion explains Germany's right to colonies.

18 October 1936

In the Kunsthalle admires Philips Wouwermann's *Dünenlandschaft mit Reiter*, Aert van der Neer's *Fluß im Mondlicht*, Hinrik Funhof's *Maria im Ährenkleid* and Piazzezza's *Die Eingeschlafene Hirtin* [now ascribed to Domenico Maggiotto]. During dinner feels his German to be insufficient.

19 October 1936

Visits Petrikirche. Inspects German grammar books in booksellers Dörling and Boysen.

20 October 1936

Claudia Asher lends him Ernst Wiechert's *Das Spiel vom Deutschen Bettelmann* and Wilhelm Müseler's *Deutsche Kunst im Wandel der Zeit*. She also recommends Hans Pferdmenges's *Deutschlands Leben* and the authors Konrad Beste and Friedrich Griebe. Reads the Wiechert that night but finds it tedious.

21 October 1936

Disparages German romantic painting in Kunsthalle. Fellow lodger recommends Anton Springer's *Geschichte der deutschen Malerei* and Eduard Fuchs's *Illustrierte Sittengeschichte*.

22 October 1936

Studies German language. After visiting Klopstockhaus and Brahms' birth house, goes with Claudia Asher to bookseller Boysens. Here he is told that histories of literature and art published before Nazis came to power are not recommended, and conversation turns to Thomas Mann's controversial *Joseph und seine Brüder*. Inspects books by Gottfried Keller and buys Karl Heinemann's *Die deutsche Dichtung; Grundriß der deutschen Literaturgeschichte*. At Pension hears that books by banned authors are difficult to obtain.

23 October 1936

Looks at nineteenth-century German and French painting, as well as German Expressionist (such as Heckel, Kirchner, Schmidt-Rottluff) works in the Kunsthalle. George Reavey writes that London publisher Nott will take *Murphy* if an American publisher could be found.

24 October 1936

Reads about the 'Moskauer Judenklique' (Moscow Jewish conspiracy). With Asher sees film *Der Verräter*. She asks him to translate an article in the *British Journal of Physical Medicine* on 'The Car and its Driver'. She tells him to embrace the new spirit in Germany; he responds by stating his intention to buy the complete works of Schopenhauer.

25 October 1936

At luncheon at the home of art collectors Helene and Cäsar Fera meets Jewish Professor Diederich, author of biographies on Zola and Daudet; they talk about Thomas Mann. Beckett inspects two literary histories: Werner Mahrholz, *Deutsche Literatur der Gegenwart*, and Wilhelm Scherer, *Geschichte der deutschen Literatur*. Visits Ohlsdorf cemetery, which he likes tremendously; does not succeed in writing a poem although the atmosphere inspires him.

26 October 1936

Visits exhibition 'Bücher der Neuen Zeit' (contemporary books) at Kupfersaal in Kunsthalle, where he inspects books by Nazi-approved authors, such as Hans Heyse's *Idee und Existenz* and Hans Grimm's *Volk ohne Raum*. Visits Helene Fera. Goes to lecture by Wilhelm Schäfer, but it has been cancelled. To cinema: *Botschaft an Garcia*.

27 October 1936

Buys German grammar book by Otto Sauer. With Hoppe goes to a meeting of the Nordische Gesellschaft (Nordic Society). Considers going out to aid when bad weather sinks lightship. Works at translation for Asher.

28 October 1936

In Staatsbibliothek looks at Karl Goedeke, *Grundriß zur Geschichte der deutschen Dichtung*; Adolf Bartels, *Handbuch zur Geschichte der deutschen Literatur* (*Eine Ergänzung meiner Literaturgeschichte*) and Anton Springer's *Handbuch der Kunstgeschichte*. Subsequently buys in Saucke book shop Curt Götz's *Dr. Med. Hiob Präterius*, Ernst Wiechert's *Todeskandidat* and Rainer Maria Rilke's *Die Weise von Liebe und Tod des Cornets Christoph Rilke*. Hears that books by Thomas Mann can still be bought, but not works by Heinrich

Mann, Arnold Zweig or Stefan Zweig. In the evening listens to broadcasts about Four-Year Plan by Hitler and Göring.

29 October 1936

Continues work on translation for Asher and reads Müseler's *Deutsche Kunst*. Visits Margaritha Durrieu and looks at her modern art collection. She shows him Herbert Read's *Art Now* and Max Sauerlandt's *Die Kunst der letzten 30 Jahre*; Beckett condemns the fact that the latter book is banned. Fellow lodger Schön lends Beckett nine contemporary books, including Rilke's *Ausgewählte Gedichte*.

30 October 1936

In Kunsthalle looks, with little interest, at contemporary Hamburg painters, but then admires Cézanne's *Am Quai de Bercy in Paris*. Buys *Katalog der neueren Meister* of Kunsthalle (compiled by Gustav Pauli). In evening listens to a speech by Hitler celebrating tenth anniversary of Berlin Gau of NSDAP. Decides to write an article on Ohlsdorf cemetery.

31 October 1936

Studies German grammar. In evening reads Rilke's *Cornet*. First reference to Beckett's new (later abandoned) work *Journal of a Melancholic*.

1 November 1936

To Kunsthalle with Claudia Asher; looks mainly at Modern Germans (he praises in particular Schmidt-Rottluff's *Patrokluskirche*) and Dutch painting. In discussion with Asher he speaks of object–subject relationship. Reads 'Reichszeitung der deutschen Erzieher' and condemns its anti-bolshevist propaganda. Notes his distaste for Asher's national socialist and anti-semitic views. Starts reading Wiechert's *Hirtennovelle*.

2 November 1936

In Saucke book shop orders Hans Pferdmenges's *Deutschlands Leben*, Ernst Barlach's *Zeichnungen* and the complete works of Schopenhauer. Conversation with Saucke and assistant Günter Albrecht about Kunsthalle and banned books such as Sauerlandt's *Die Kunst der letzten 30 Jahre*. Evening with Asher, who corrects Beckett's German translation of the poem 'Cascando'.

3 November 1936
Day excursion to Lübeck; visits Dom, Marienkirche and other sights.

4 November 1936
Compares the stairs in the Elbtunnel with scenes in German expressionist films. Then picks up books ordered at Saucke, and also buys Paul Alverdes's novel *Pfeiferstube*. Conversation with Albrecht about the literary magazines *Querschnitt* and *Das Innere Reich*.

5 November 1936
Realises that Pferdmenges's *Deutschlands Leben* is Nazi propaganda; reads article on Goethe in *Frankfurter Zeitung*. Then to Staatsbibliothek to read two books on the Ohlsdorf cemetery.

6 November 1936
Spends day in Blankenese, taking in Bismarck Park and Süllberg. In evening meets Günter Albrecht; they discuss mainly literature (Hesse, Mann, Alverdes, Hamsun, Proust), art and political issues. Hears about lecture series 'Volkhafte Dichtung der Zeit' (Stehr, Berens–Totenohl, Weinheber). They also discuss (and criticise) Wiechert's *Hirtennovelle* and Rudolf Binding's *Waffenbrüder*.

7 November 1936
Buys 1932 edition of Grieben's guide to Hamburg, and then goes on extensive walk through outskirts.

8 November 1936
Asked by the Pension's maid Emmy to compose a poem for her boyfriend.

9 November 1936
Returns to Ohlsdorf cemetery, then goes to Saucke. Looks at Georg Dehio's *Handbuch der deutschen Kunst* in 4 volumes, and other art books (Bosch and Brueghel). Buys Erwin Guido Kolbenheyer's Spinoza novel *Amor Dei*. Finishes Binding's *Waffenbrüder* in the evening.

10 November 1936
Spends afternoon at the Durrieus; he looks at their art collection and discusses the forthcoming ban of books by Barlach and Nolde. Margaritha Durrieu arranges a meeting for Beckett with Jewish art

historian Rosa Schapire. Following a reading by Hermann Stehr in the evening he deems the story *Der Schatten* too sentimental.

11 November 1936
On way to Kunsthalle with Margaritha Durrieu encounter Hildebrandt Gurlitt (of Kunstverein Rabenstraße). At the gallery they look at Dutch, German romantic, French and contemporary local painting.

12 November 1936
Attends lecture by Professor von Mercklin in Museum für Kunst und Gewerbe on the 'Geometric Period'. Then buys (at Saucke's book shop) Emil Nolde's autobiography *Das eigene Leben*; Paul Alverdes's *Reinhold im Dienst*; the anthology *Älteste deutsche Dichtungen*, and the recent issue of the journal *Das Innere Reich*, which had been banned for some time. Instead of a (cancelled) lecture on the Italian Renaissance, Beckett and Margaritha Durrieu attend a lecture by Lucien Brulez on Diderot; they subsequently discuss Proust with Brulez.

13 November 1936
In a letter to George Reavey rejects demands by Houghton Mifflin to cut *Murphy* and sends image of apes playing chess as potential cover for book. In Kunstverein Rabenstraße finds Beckmann's use of colour interesting, and subsequently inspects Hildebrand Gurlitt's private collection of modern art. Hears about Peter Dülberg exhibition at Gallery Lüders. Visits Ilse Schneider, who lends him Franz Werfel's *Verdi*. In the evening listens to radio broadcast of concert by British Philharmonic Orchestra playing in Berlin.

14 November 1936
Views Rosa Schapire's extensive Schmidt-Rottluff collection at her home. At Saucke purchases *Sprüche, Lieder, der Leich. Urtext und Prosaübertragung* by Walther von der Vogelweide. Meets Albrecht; they discuss the banning of Franz Marc and Franz Werfel. Finishes reading Alverdes's *Pfeiferstube*, which he judges to be very good.

15 November 1936
Works on the German translation of his poem 'Cascando' with Rosa Schapire. They discuss her prohibition to publish and work

as art historian, sanctions against 'degenerate' modern art, and the
work of the philosopher Johan Huizinga. Asked to comment on a
portrait of Schapire by Schmidt-Rottluff, Beckett described it as art
as prayer, which in turn provokes prayer in perceiver.

16 November 1936
Goes to the Peter Dülberg exhibition at the Gallery Lüders
with Margaritha Durrieu, and finds the pictures too sentimental.
Inspects books by Huizinga and Windelband at Saucke's book
shop. In the evening hears that Russians have mobilised on Polish
border and have arrested German citizens. At the cinema sees the
film *Meuterei*.

17 November 1936
Together with Margaritha Durrieu at the Museum für Kunst und
Gewerbe; the custodian Kurt Dingelstedt declares that works by
Schmidt-Rottluff cannot be seen. Albrecht informs Beckett that
his bookseller friend Axel Kaun would like to meet him. Fails to
compose poem for Emmy.

18 November 1936
Studies German vocabulary and finishes reading, without pleasure,
Henry von Heiseler's *Wawas Ende*.

19 November 1936
Beckett is impressed by the drawings of Schmidt-Rottluff and
Ludwig Kirchner in the Kupferstichkabinett. By chance meets
Schapire, who manages to get Beckett access to the cellar in
order to see 'degenerate' pictures removed from Kunsthalle. Here
he views Expressionist paintings by Schmidt-Rottluff, Kirchner,
Nolde, Pechstein and Kokoschka's *Windsbraut*. He is particularly
impressed by Nolde's *Christus und die Kinder*. He does not have
time to see paintings by Liebermann locked away in another
room. In conversation with the custodian he praises Ingres and
Wouwermann but disparages Philip Otto Runge. Back in the
reading room of the Kupferstichkabinett reads about 'Brücke'
movement in Max Deri's *Neue Malerei* and inspects Franz Marc's
Briefe, Aufzeichnungen und Aphorismen. From Marc's book he
transcribes passages dealing with alienation of subject (artist) from
object (art work) and with Marc's intent to paint the predicate
of living. In the evening attends a lecture by Brulez, who in

subsequent discussion reveals his reservations about Beckett's study *Proust*. He meets Irma Tiedtke, who has written the doctoral thesis *Symbole und Bilder im Werke Marcel Prousts*. With Asher sees the film *Frau ohne Bedeutung* with Gustav Gründgens.

20 November 1936
Finds the academic style of Tiedtke's thesis tedious. Goes to concert by the Berlin Philharmonic with Ilse Schneider; he admires Strauss's *Don Quixote* as well as the rendition of Bolero and Brahms's 2nd Symphony. They have dinner in the Jewish restaurant Halali, and discuss music and Nuremberg sculpture. Beckett disparages historical art. Writes a short essay in German on Brahms in his diary.

21 November 1936
Visits the widow and son of the art historian (and previous director of the Museum für Kunst und Gewerbe) Max Sauerlandt; viewing the family's private art collection, Beckett again praises Kirchner and Schmidt-Rottluff. They allow him to buy a copy of Sauerlandt's prohibited book *Die Kunst der letzten 30 Jahre*. Spends evening in St. Pauli with Asher, who presents him with a copy of Hugo von Hofmannsthal's *Der Tor und der Tod*.

22 November 1936
Together with Rosa Schapire views the private art collection of Heinrich C. Hudtwalcker, and is particularly impressed by Edvard Munch's *Mädchen auf der Brücke* and paintings by Otto Müller. Learns of closure of modern wing in Kronprinzenpalais (Berlin). Then with Margaritha Durrieu to Kunstverein for a (boring) lecture by the painter Friedrich Ahlers-Hestermann. Talks with artist Peter Dülberg. At dinner in home of the Durrieus hears how Hans Grimm's *Volk ohne Raum* epitomises the new times more than Thomas Mann. Continues reading Werfel's *Verdi*.

23 November 1936
Deems the story of Hofmannsthal's *Der Tor und der Tod* simplistic but notes lines he admires. Sits as model at Margaritha Durrieu's drawing session, but finds results disappointing. Meets the painters Ahlers-Hestermann and Karl Kluth. Conversation once again circles around the closure of the modern wing in the Berlin

Kronprinzenpalais, and the fact that Alfred Rosenberg is the main enemy of modern art in Germany.

24 November 1936
Margaritha Durrieu introduces Beckett to the Jewish artist Gretchen Wohlwill, who describes Nazi persecutions and her prohibition to paint. Continues to read Werfel's *Verdi*.

25 November 1936
Visits painter Karl Kluth in his studio; detects influence of Munch and the antithesis of the natural and the human. Afterwards visits Willem Grimm (whom Beckett admires most of the contemporary Hamburg painters) in Uhlendorferpalais, where he also meets the sculptor Hans Martin Ruwoldt and Gretchen Wohlwill. In a pub later with Grimm meets the painter Karl Ballmer and his wife; in a radio broadcast Goebbels announces Germany's treaty with Japan against Communism.

26 November 1936
Irma Tiedtke criticises Beckett's *Proust* in a letter. Impressed by Karl Ballmer's paintings when visiting the artist's studio; he interprets Ballmer as metaphysical and concrete rather than abstract, and invokes Leibniz's monadology and his own poem 'The Vulture'. Beckett notes Ballmer's apolitical attitude in the face of restrictions imposed by the Nazis since 1933. At Sauerlandts looks at their private collection again; he is given the addresses of Nolde, Heckel and Schmidt-Rottluff in Berlin. Then with Margaritha Durrieu to Eduard Bargheer's studio; hears of the painter's difficulties with authorities. Defines movement as the prime theme of Bargheer's painting and admires his energy, but prefers the reticence and the unsaid of Ballmer and Grimm.

27 November 1936
Decides to write a poem on theme of the 'Paternoster', with reference to Heraclitus. Reads Sauerlandt's discussion of Ballmer.

28 November 1936
Reads more Tiedtke, but regrets the fact that Proust as artist is lost in the academic jargon.

29 November 1936
With Margaritha Durrieu sees a theatre performance of Martin Rabe's *Der Unentbehrliche* in Thalia–Theater. Then to Günter Albrecht's home for dinner.

30 November 1936
With Willem Grimm visits Karl Ballmer in Glinde; the artists Ruwoldt and Bollmann also there. Together they go to a boxing event.

1 December 1936
Endeavours to get permission to see banned art works in the Kunsthalle.

2 December 1936
Receives letter of recommendation from British Consulate to see banned art works (too late to use). At the Durrieus meets the journalist Greven. Margaritha Durrieu asks Beckett not to publish any disparagements of Germany as this could result in repercussions for people he has met.

3 December 1936
Instructs Saucke's book shop to send 20 books to Dublin [cf. 'Whoroscope' notebook]. Also orders Huizinga's *Holland* and Windelband's *Geschichte der Philosophie*. Runs into Peter Dülberg on way to his leaving party at lodgings.

4 December 1936
Spends day in **Lüneburg** looking at churches before travelling on to **Hannover**.

5 December 1936
Admires the work of Tilman Riemenschneider and Hans Baldung Grien in Hannover's Provinzialmuseum and visits the Leibnizhaus before taking train to **Braunschweig**.

6 December 1936
Visits the Martinikirche, Rathaus, Gewandhaus, Dom, and Burg Dankwarderode. Finds much to praise in the art gallery, the Herzog Anton Ulrich Museum, in particular Giorgione's *Self-Portrait*. Reads Sauerlandt's chapter on Nolde.

7 December 1936
Excursion to **Riddagshausen** to visit the Frauenkapelle and the
Klosterkirche. Back in Braunschweig goes to cinema: *Wenn wir alle
Engel wären.*

8 December 1936
To Herzog Anton Ulrich Museum; studies facial expression of
Giorgione's *Self-Portrait*. Then to **Wolfenbüttel**, visiting the Schloss,
the Hauptkirche and the two Lessing houses. Buys complete works
of Lessing. In Augusta Bibliothek, where Lessing was librarian,
reads first part of the *Wolfenbütteler Fragmente*, which advocates a
religion based on reason.

9 December 1936
Herzog Anton Ulrich Museum. Climbs up tower of Andreaskirche.

10 December 1936
Day excursion to **Hildesheim**, visits the Michaeliskirche, the Dom
and other historical buildings.

11 December 1936
Decides not to visit Königsluther and travels on to **Berlin**. Initially
stays at Hotel Deutsche Traube. Reads in paper of Edward VIII's
abdication .

12–15 December 1936
Extensive exploratory walks through Berlin, and first visits to the
Kaiser Friedrich and the Tell Halaf museums. Buys Grieben guide
to Berlin.

16–17 December 1936
In Kaiser Friedrich Museum studies Italian Old Masters (praising
in particular Andrea del Sarto and Signorelli) and the Flemish and
Dutch collections. Admires a night landscape by Adam Elsheimer
in loan exhibition of drawings from the Louvre. Moves into Pension
Kempt.

18 December 1936
Looks at German painting in the Deutsches Museum. Singles out
Dürer's portraits of Jacob Muffel and Hieronymus Holzschuher,
Hans Multscher's panels for the Wurzacher Altar and discovers

Albrecht Altdorfer. In loan exhibition inspects the Elsheimer night landscape again, as well as drawings by Dürer.

19 December 1936
In Kronprinzenpalais looks at modern paintings, praising Kokoschka's portrait of Adolf Loos and works by Munch; denigrates the current 'Sittenaustellung' [exhibition of 'customs']. In the drawing collection looks at dossiers by Schmidt-Rottluff and Kirchner, preferring the latter's work to Schmidt-Rottluff's monumentalism. As expected finds the upper gallery wings closed; notes in diary the contradictory Nazi cultural politics in allowing drawings by discredited painters to be seen when paintings of the same have been removed from walls.

20 December 1936
Italians in the Kaiser Friedrich Museum from Giotto to Giorgione, noting particularly Masaccio's work and Domenico Veneziano's *Adoration of the Kings*. Meets friends of Claudia Asher, and criticises their National Socialist views.

21 December 1936
First long visit to Tell Halaf Museum. Then Nationalgalerie; not impressed by collections of nineteenth-century German and French art. Spends evening with Rosa Schapire discussing abstract and metaphysical art.

22 December 1936
Vorderasiatisches Museum.

23 December 1936
Top floor of Nationalgalerie; nineteenth-century German art.

24–25 December 1936
Long walks in outskirts of Berlin (Charlottenburger Schloß, Grünewald, and Wannsee). Finishes reading Alverdes's *Reinhold im Dienst* (prefers his *Pfeiferstube*). Reads Heinemann on Wedekind.

26 December 1936
Visits Pergamon, Neues and Vorderasiatisches museums, showing interest in the latter's collection of Islamic art and Indian miniatures. Walks to Bellevue Schloß.

27 December 1936
To Altes Museum, then long walk along the river Spree.

28 December 1936
Looks at nineteenth-century German paintings in the National-galerie without much enthusiasm. Buys Gottfried Keller's *Der grüne Heinrich*, and proceeds to read first chapter. Continues work on creative piece, presumably the *Journal of a Melancholic*.

29 December 1936
Italians in the Kaiser Friedrich Museum, finding much to admire. Reading *Der grüne Heinrich*.

30 December 1936
Kaiser Friedrich Museum, with focus on Brouwers, Rubens, van Dyck, Teniers, and French collection. Later to Humboldt-Hafen.

31 December 1936
Walks through Tiergarten and along Spree. In evening dragged out to New Year festivities by landlord Kempt.

1 January 1937
Work on new creative project. In cinema sees the film *San Francisco*.

2 January 1937
Continues work. Then to Kaiser Friedrich Museum to study paintings by Dutch School. Goes to the theatre in the evening.

3–4 January 1937
Explores Berlin.

5 January 1937
Studies the Dutch and Flemish collections in the Kaiser Friedrich Museum; impressed by Gerard Terborch's *Die Familie des Schleifers*. Buys a copy of Friedrich Schiller's *Maria Stuart*. Then with landlord Kempt and the actor Eichheim to watch the film *Der lachende Dritte*, in which Eichheim plays.

6 January 1937
Reads *Maria Stuart*. In long conversation landlord Kempt explains the reasons for his anti-semitism and praises the Nazi interior minister Wilhelm Frick.

7 January 1937
Views with interest the Egyptian collection in the Neues Museum.
Buys Frederick the Great's text *Über die deutsche Literatur*. With
Kempt and Eichheim to see latter in the film *Der Jäger von Fall*.
Continues reading *Maria Stuart*, finding Schiller's style of writing
less humane and more sentimental than Goethe's.

8 January 1937
Kaiser Friedrich Museum: late Florence, North Italian schools and
Boticelli; admires in particular Andrea del Sarto's *Virgin Enthroned
with Child and 8 Saints*, and Piero Pollaiuolo's *Annunciation*. Buys
Wilhelm Fraenger's *Matthias Grünewald in seinen Werken*, and
Friedrich Hebbel's *Gyges und sein Ring*. Finishes reading Schiller's
Maria Stuart, before going to Staatstheater to see production of the
play.

9–10 January 1937
Reads Hebbel's *Gyges und sein Ring* and goes to the cinema to see
the film *Burgtheater* with the actor Karl Kraus.

11 January 1937
In the Nationalgalerie looks at paintings by German romantics
and French. Buys Friedrich Hebbel's *Gedichte* in 5 volumes. Spends
the evening with Axel Kaun, whose criticisms of the Nazi regime
he finds insightful. Notes Kaun's opinion that the Russians see
Goebbels as their advocate in Germany, and regrets the failure of
Jews in exile to mount 'spiritual' criticism. Beckett also learns from
Kaun that Thomas Mann's works are now definitely banned and
that the author has been stripped of his German citizenship.

12 January 1937
In an excursion to Potsdam he visits the Sanssouci Palace with
its Voltaire room and gallery. To the theatre in the evening for
a performance of Hebbel's *Gyges und sein Ring*. Notes that the
poetical play doomed to fail because the poetry obscures the drama
and is in turn obscured by drama.

13 January 1937
Flemish Collection in the Kaiser Friedrich Museum. In the evening
performance of Beethoven's *Leonore* by the Berlin Philharmonic.

14 January 1937
Reads *Der grüne Heinrich*, finding it tedious.

15 January 1937
On recommendation of Kaun purchases Friedrich Stieve's *Abriß der deutschen Geschichte von 1792–1935*, but notes with dismay that it is not a reference book as he had hoped, but a book that, to his mind, propounds German destiny. He reads about the new Glaspalast in Munich, and the forthcoming exhibition of Nazi art in the Haus der deutschen Kunst; responds with disgust at the statement that the decadence of Nolde, Munch etc. has been defeated by the Nazis. Spends the evening with Kaun, who presents him with a copy of Knut Hamsun's *Der Ring schließt sich* and lends him various contemporary novels. In conversation Beckett denies the validity of a deterministic view of history as evidenced in ideas of a 'German destiny'. Against modern animism and rationality he sets the concepts of chance and incoherence. They also discuss the poet Rainer Maria Rilke and Edvard Munch's painting.

16 January 1937
Meets Günter Albrecht on his way through Berlin.

17 January 1937
Reads Walter Bauer's *Die Notwendige Reise*.

18 January 1937
Reading Hermann Hesse's *Demian*, which he enjoys but criticises for its lack of sincerity. Notes as characteristic of modern German literature the journey of discovery, to the self, God or 'us' and contrasts this with Murphy's lack of movement.

19 January 1937
The landlord Kempt relates the development of National Socialism, starting with the 9 November 1923 demonstration. Beckett notes his agreement with Kaun's analysis of the NSDAP, with Goebbels being the central figure while Hitler and Goering are the popular and sentimental figures in the foreground. Continues reading *Demian*.

20 January 1937

Exchanges Stieve's book for Karl Scheffler's *Deutsche Maler und Zeichner im 19. Jahrhundert*. To Kronprinzenpalais, where he admires paintings by van Gogh and Munch. Analyses the tendency of Nordic artists such as Munch, Nolde and Hamsun to sentimentalise the emotional world, and states belief that pity does not produce good art.

21 January 1937

Finishes reading *Demian* and criticises the 'Traumbild' (dream passage). Looks at German Masters in the Deutsches Museum, especially Konrad Witz, Albrecht Dürer and Multscher. Buys a book with Flemish and German reproductions, and Grieben guides for Weimar and Leipzig. In the evening he meets the stage designer Porep (Staatstheater in Halle).

22 January 1937

Leaves Berlin for **Halle** and spends the evening with Porep.

23 January 1937

Goes to Moritzburg to see a so-called 'Schreckenskammer', a special exhibition of 'decadent' modern art. Beckett is impressed by the mostly Expressionist works by Heckel, Klee, Marc, Kokoschka, Kirchner, Kandinsky, Feiniger, Munch, Müller and Schmidt-Rottluff. (This collection of modern art, assembled by Sauerlandt, was integrated nearly in entirety in the 'Entartete Kunst' exhibition in Munich later that year.) Afterwards goes to see Felix Weise's private modern art collection (mainly Kirchner); conversation with Weise's wife about the creative and material difficulties faced by young artists in Nazi Germany. Before travelling on to **Weimar** meets Porep and buys Hermann Giesau's book on the Naumburger Dom.

24 January 1937

After a brief walk around Weimar goes to **Erfurt** for the day. Visits the gallery where modern paintings still on view, but also inspects German Old Masters and nineteenth-century painters. Judges the Erfurt Dom to be the best example of Gothic architecture he has seen. Back in Weimar witnesses a Nazi party in the

Stadthausrestaurant, and hears the song 'Ein Hund kam in die Küche' [cf. *Waiting for Godot*].

25 January 1937
Visits main attractions in Weimar: Goethehaus; Schillerhaus; Fürstenhaus; Schloß–Museum (with gallery); Wittumspalais. Notes that apparently Max Klinger, Friedrich Nietzsche and Richard Wagner are the official representatives of Nazi art. In evening leaves Weimar for **Naumburg**.

26 January 1937
Inspects with enthusiasm the interior of the Naumburger Dom; he is particularly impressed by the West Screen, which he interprets as being psychological rather than religious. Travels on by train to **Leipzig**.

27 January 1937
In Leipzig Kunstmuseum admires paintings by Melchior Feselen, Frans Hals and David Teniers, but finds the large Max Klinger exhibition horrendous. Reads *Goethe und seine Welt* (ed. by Anton Kippenberg and Hans Wahl).

28 January 1937
Returns to the art gallery; paintings by the 'decadent' artists Nolde, Heckel and Pechstein have been removed. Looks instead at Dutch and Flemish collections.

29 January 1937
Travels on to **Dresden**; walks around the city and looks at Landtagsgebäude, Alte Akademie (containing Neue Staatliche Gemäldegalerie), Akademie der Bildenden Künste, the Albertinum, Augustusbrücke, Propsteikirche, the Opera and the Zwinger Courtyard.

30 January 1937
At the hotel listens to a radio broadcast for three hours with speeches by Hitler and Göring at the opening of the Reichstag. Moves into the Pension Höfer.

31 January 1937
Whilst inspecting nineteenth-century paintings in the Alte Akademie comes across Kaspar David Friedrich's *Zwei Männer in*

Betrachtung des Mondes. Sightseeing. Reads an unspecified text by Hitler, and later borrows the anthology *Rainer Maria Rilke: Stimmen der Freunde; Ein Gedächtnisbuch* from his landlord Höfer.

1 February 1937
In Gemäldegalerie looks at Italian Masters. Judges something to be wrong with the left leg of Giorgione's *Sleeping Venus*. Admires in particular Antonello's *St. Sebastian*, but also Titian's *Virgin and Child* and Raphael's *Sistine Madonna*. Leaves letter of introduction from Porep at the home of the dancer Gret Palucca, step-daughter of the art collector Ida Bienert.

2 February 1937
Concentrates on Old Masters at Gemäldegalerie and shows particular interest in Rembrandt's *Samson's Wedding*, Vermeer's *Die Kupplerin*, as well as Dürer's *Portrait of a Young Man*. Then visits the art historian Will Grohmann, and looks at his private art collection and fine art library. Grohmann explains his interest in Klee, Picasso and Kandinsky, and they agree that Kirchner is the best of the 'Brücke' painters. They discuss the situation of modern art within Nazi Germany, and Grohmann relates how he has been released from professional positions by the authorities. Nevertheless the art historian refuses to think of going into exile and states his belief that it is important that intellectuals prepare for the collapse of the regime within Germany.

3 February 1937
To modern wing of the Gemäldegalerie: beyond paintings by Kokoschka, Nolde, Hofer, Munch and Dix collection comprised mainly of nineteenth-century German painting. Notes his surprise that Liebermann pictures still hanging here. With help of 1930 catalogue he establishes which paintings have been removed by the Nazis. Reads Da Ponte's edition of *Marriage of Figaro* in German translation and attends performance of the play in the evening at the opera.

4 February 1937
Hears that the publishers Dent and Cobden Sanderson have turned down *Murphy*.

5 February 1937
Looks at the Dutch and Flemish collections in the Gemäldegalerie, paying particular attention to paintings by Brouwers, Wouwerman's landscapes and Vermeer's *Lesendes Mädchen*. Buys German–Italian edition of *Marriage of Figaro* and *Don Giovanni*. Attends dinner party at Friedrich Bienert (the son of Ida Bienert), and meets Russian *emigrés* such as Prince Obolensky and the von Gersdorffs.

6 February 1937
Meets the director of the Gemäldegalerie, Hans Posse, who advises Beckett that removed paintings are not to be seen (most had been removed from site or returned to owners).

7 February 1937
On reading Voltaire's *Candide* and Renard's *Journal* expresses admiration for French culture. Visits Ida Bienert and is shown her extensive and important private collection of modern art; he is particularly impressed by a non-abstract painting by Kandinsky and a work by Cézanne. Starts writing a poem beginning 'always elsewhere', but abandons it after three lines.

8 February 1937
Wanders through town in the snow. Reads Scheffler on the Nazarener school of art.

9 February 1937
Visits the Zwinger Print Room, before going on to the Gemäldegalerie to look at the Italian Masters; inspects Giorgione's *Sleeping Venus* again and praises Poussin's *Venus*. Then in French Pavillion admires the Watteaus.

10 February 1937
Finds a lot to admire in paintings by Rembrandt and Dürer in the Gemäldegalerie. Reads article by Giesau in *Dresdner Nachrichten* on the attribution of statues in Meißner and Naumburger cathedrals. To Japanisches Palais to hear Prince Obolensky lecture on the Italian Renaissance, and joins subsequent party. Notes that Jungian psychoanalysis is tolerated in Germany and has replaced Freud in importance.

11 February 1937

After a walk in the city meets Grohmann; their conversation revolves around Ireland and modern German art. Grohmann explains the restoration history of the Giorgione, and compares the antithetical methods employed by Joyce, Klee and Picasso in their work. On invitation by Friedrich Bienert attends a concert by the Quartetto di Roma performing Mozart, Verdi and Beethoven.

12 February 1937

With exception of Gide's contribution expresses disappointment with the commemorative anthology *Rilke – Stimmen der Freunde*. Goes to Meißen for the day, visiting the Dom and the Albrechtsburg; finds a tour of the porcelain factory disappointing.

13 February 1937

Spends the day trying to sell his leather coat in several Jewish pawn shops. In Gemäldegalerie studies once again Italian Old Masters, and comments favourably on Mantegna's *Holy Family* and two Ercole de' Roberti paintings. The gallery's director, Hans Posse, shows him the x-ray of Giorgione's *Sleeping Venus*, which reveals restoration work.

14 February 1937

At the Alte Akademie Beckett studies the French collection (admiring Renoir), the works of Van Gogh and finally nineteenth-century German paintings (once again paying attention to Kaspar David Friedrich). Reads Scheffler on Friedrich, Runge, Rothel and Böcklin.

15 February 1937

Visits Ida Bienert again to study her art collection, singling out Kandinsky's *Träumerische Improvisation*. She presents him with Will Grohmann's catalogue of her collection, on condition he keep it hidden whilst in Germany. Dinner with the von Gersdorffs.

16 February 1937

To Pillnitz, where he visits the castle and the various palaces before walking via Melxmühle to Borsberg.

17 February 1937

Dutch, Flemish and Italian collections at the Gemäldegalerie; studies in particular Adriaen van der Velde, Brouwer and the

Vermeer *Kupplerin*. Whilst looking at Antonello's *St Sebastian* thinks of writing a poem. Watches the film *Der Hund von Baskerville* at the cinema.

18 February 1937
Goes to the Gemäldegalerie for the last time; inspects Matthias Grünewald drawings and notes locations of his work across Germany and Switzerland. Has a last look at the Antonello and the Vermeer. Notices in an article on Klinger in the *Leipziger Anzeiger* the argument that Liebermann is not a German artist because he is preoccupied with the object in his paintings. In the evening attends a lecture by Fedor Stepun on the Russian writer Andreiev Belii.

19 February 1937
Leaves Dresden for **Freiberg** where he inspects the porch of the cathedral, the Goldne Pforte. Then on to **Bamberg**.

20–21 February 1937
Visits various churches and historical buildings but spends most of these two days looking at the cathedral, admiring the Bamberger Reiter, the Fürstenportal and the Georgenchor.

22 February 1937
Takes the train to Staffelstein, then walks via Schloß Banz to the Vierzehnheiligen Church. Beckett's reference to the painter Liebermann in a pub provokes anti-semitic comments.

23 February 1937
The Neue Residenz and its gallery as well as the cathedral (the Bamberger Dom) are once again on Beckett's programme. He reads a newspaper article by Goebbels.

24 February 1937
Inspects bibles, Dürer copper prints and an edition of Dürer's *Niederländisches Tagebuch* at the library (Staatsbibliothek). Visits the Dom again. Then travels on to **Würzburg**. Buys a guide book by Fritz Knapp, which he reads in the evening.

25 February 1937
Sightseeing: Würzburger Residenz, Fränkisches Leopold Museum (where he admires sculptures by Tilman Riemenscheider and the

work of the so-called Wohlfskehlmeister), Marienkapelle and the Kiliansdom. Reads Knapp in the evening.

26 February 1937

Visits the Neumünsterkirche and the adjoining Lusamgärtchen with Walther von der Vogelweide's tomb. Leaves Würzburg by train for **Nürnberg**.

27 February 1937

Buys Grieben guide to Nürnberg. Sightseeing, with the highlight being the Sebalduskirche which contains Kraft's Schreyersches Grabmal, the Sebaldus Grab by Vischer, the Loeffelholzkapelle, the Halleraltar by the Master of the Tucheraltar and the Tuchersche Tafel by Kulmbach. Spends the afternoon in the Germanisches Museum where he admires an *Annunciation* by Konrad Witz.

28 February 1937

Returns to the Germanisches Museum. Notes his thoughts on the main Nuremberg period (1470–1530) with work by sculptors such as Vischer, Pleydenwurff, Stoss, Riemenschneider and Kraft. Reads Hans Carossa's *Geheimniße des reifen Lebens*.

1 March 1937

Further visits to churches, focusing on sculptures such as the Pergenstörfferisches Grabmal by Adam Kraft. Compiles a list of works and their locations in Nürnberg by Veit Stoss, Peter Vischer and Adam Kraft. Continues reading Carossa, commenting on his use of Dante.

2 March 1937

After visiting the Heiliggeistspital (now an old people's home), inspired to sketch a short poem. Visits the torture chamber in the castle [mentioned in *Dream*]. Travels on to **Regensburg**.

3 March 1937

Visits the Regensburger Dom and other churches and historical buildings. Buys a selection of Georg Trakl's poetry and Richard Wiebel's study of the Schottentor (northern door of the cathedral).Wanders in grounds of Thurn und Taxis estate.

4 March 1937
Goes back to the Schottentor of the Dom, then on to the various chapels on the Thurn und Taxis estate. Travels onward to **Munich**.

5 March 1937
Moves into lodgings at the Pension Romana; spends the evening sampling the various beer houses, including the Hofbräuhaus. A compositor who admires Hitler shows Beckett where the demonstrating Nazis were shot in November 1923.

6–7 March 1937
Exploratory walks around Munich. Sees the Austrian film *Premiere*.

8 March 1937
First visit to the Alte Pinakothek to look at Italian collection; judges it to be less good than the one in the Kaiser Friedrich Museum in Berlin. He still finds plenty to praise, for example Antonello da Messina's *Virgin of the Annunciation*.

9 March 1937
Back to the Alte Pinakothek; German and Flemish painting. He is impressed by Dierick Bouts the Elder's *Resurrection*, and shows particular interest in Grünewald and Gabriel Mäleskircher. Sitting on steps of Glypthothek in Königsplatz ponders the new Nazi architecture around the square. Armed with letters of introduction by Porep and Ida Bienert contacts the dentist Dr Zarnitz and Hans von Rupé (custodian at the Bayerisches Nationalmuseum).

10 March 1937
Meets Rupé at the Bayerisches Nationalmuseum. They agree that the Nazi architecture on the Königsplatz lacks creativity. Beckett reads Hitler's aphorisms inscribed on the Haus der deutschen Kunst.

11 March 1937
Lunch at Rupé's home. They discuss Rilke, Proust and the inadequacies of language. Beckett argues that the French language enables stylelessness, and praises the painters Ballmer and Mäleskircher. Early evening meets Zarnitz and his circle of friends, amongst which the painter Achmann and the bookseller Severing.

Topics of conversation include art (Mäleskircher) and literature (Alverdes, Stifter, Trakl and Bunyan).

12 March 1937

Inspects, in Severing's book shop, Georg Dehio's *Geschichte der Deutschen Kunst* and a biography of Adalbert Stifter by Urban Roedl (ie Bruno Adler), and buys Stifter's *Der Nachsommer*. Conversation with Severing about various modern German writers, in particular Georg Heym. Goes to the cinema to watch the film *Etappenhase*. Finishes reading Carossa's *Geheimniße des reifen Leben* and picks up Keller's *Der grüne Heinrich* again.

13 March 1937

At the Alte Pinakothek looks at German Masters from Dürer to Rottenhammer, and notes a detailed interpretation of Dürer's *Four Apostles*. Reads *Der grüne Heinrich* but still finds it overall too slow and pedantic.

14 March 1937

Looks at the Dutch collection in the Alte Pinakothek. In the evening he goes to a performance of Karl Valentin at the Kabaret Benz.

15 March 1937

Studies nineteenth-century German paintings in the Neue Staatsgalerie. Goes to Günther Francke's art gallery, where he is shown several paintings by Max Beckmann. (Notes that Francke one of the few dealers still showing modern art.) Later attends a (to his mind disappointing) concert conducted by Furtwängler, with pieces by Mozart, Beethoven and Schumann. Continues to read (as he does over the next few days) Keller's *Der grüne Heinrich*.

16 March 1937

To Deutsches Museum with its collection of nineteenth-century German and modern art; praises Cézanne's *Railway Cutting*, Van Gogh's *Self-Portrait* and a Monet (*Pont d'Argenteuil*).

17 March 1937

Receives addresses of painters Josef Scharl, Edgar Ende and Josef Mader from Francke. Goes to Alte Pinakothek to look at the Dutch and Flemish collections. Invited to Francke's in the evening, where he meets the painter Otto Griebel; they discuss the work of Max

Beckmann and the upcoming exhibition of Nazi-approved art in the Haus der deutschen Kunst.

18 March 1937
Buys Alverdes's *Kleine Reise; Aus einem Tagebuch*. In the evening attends a theatre performance of Curt Götz's *Dr. Hiob Präterius*.

19 March 1937
Looks at the Italian and French collections at the Alte Pinakothek. Then to Edgar Ende's studio, whose surrealist paintings do not appeal. Ende criticises Dalí and Ernst but praises Joyce and Ballmer, and reveals his interest in Rudolf Steiner's anthroposophy, Goethe and German myths. Then visits the theatre director Eggers-Kestner, and views his small private art collection. They discuss Hamburg painters (with whom Eggers-Kestner familiar), Porep (as Eggers-Kestner wants to hire him as stage designer), theatre (Beckett discusses the staging of Hebbel's *Gyges und sein Ring*, Schiller's *Maria Stuart*, Jonson's *Alchemist* and *Volpone*, Machiavelli's *Mandragola*) and Barlach as playwright. Eggers-Kestner lends him two works by Karl Ballmer: *Deutschtum und Christentum in der Teosophie des Goetheanismus* and *Aber Herr Heidegger!*

20 March 1937
Reads with interest Karl Ballmer's *Aber Herr Heidegger!*, taking extensive notes in his diary. Hears that Houghton Mifflin in the US and thus also Nott in England have turned down *Murphy*.

21 March 1937
Beckett sees the propaganda film *Weiße Sklaven* at the cinema.

22 March 1937
Admires Spanish and Italian paintings in the Alte Pinakothek. Visits the bookseller Severing, who doubts he can get hold of Justi's *Von Corinth zu Klee*, nor an edition of Barlach's theatre. Inspects books by Kierkegaard and Cassirer. Reads Hans Carossa's *Führung und Geleit*.

23 March 1937
Abandons Ballmer's *Deutschtum und Christentum* due to preponderance of quotations from Rudolf Steiner. Continues reading

Carossa's *Führung und Geleit*, noting its references to Hofmannsthal, Thomas Mann and Barlach. During a visit to his studio judges Josef Mader's pictures to be poor.

24 March 1937
Looks at Greek artefacts in the Glyptothek. Finishes reading Carossa's *Führung und Geleit*.

25 March 1937
Reads Hans Carossa's *Der Arzt Dr Gion* and goes to Bayerisches Nationalmuseum, taking note of Konrad Witz's paintings.

26 March 1937
Visits Nymphenburg and then Amalienburg. Meets with Eggers-Kestner, and they discuss theatre, film, and the nature of language. Beckett explains language's inadequacy by arguing that it cannot express dissonance because it is chronological rather than simultaneous; he illustrates this by referring to Joyce's attempt to achieve musical simultaneity within *Finnegans Wake*. Eggers-Kestner rings the publisher Piper in attempt to obtain a copy of a prohibited Barlach book for Beckett.

27 March 1937
Concentrates on early German altars in a visit to the Alte Pinakothek, and notes his admiration for Mäleskircher and Marx Reichling. Carries on reading Carossa's *Gion*. Orders the autobiography *Ernst Barlach, ein selbsterzähltes Leben*.

28 March 1937
Takes the tram out to Grünwald, then walks via Straßlach and Schäftlarn to Icking. Buys Grimmelshausen's *Simplicissimus*, and finishes reading Carossa's *Gion*.

29 March 1937
Reads Friedländer's discussion of Schongauer and the Antwerp manierists. At the Alte Pinakothek studies Dutch paintings and the German Old Masters, and once again notes his thoughts on Dürer's *Four Apostles*. Spends evening with a group of people including the actor Eichheim but finds their views of films, politics and art simplistic.

30 March 1937
Piper refuses to hand over a copy of the banned Barlach, fearing recriminations should Beckett be searched at the border. Meets Paul Alverdes at Severing's bookshop; the German writer suggests Beckett should contribute to a projected English number of *Das Innere Reich*. Buys Britting's collection of short stories, *Kleine Welt am Strom*, and Grimmelshausen's *Der Abenteurliche Simplicissimus*. Meets Rupé at the Bayerisches Museum. Types up his German version of the poem 'Cascando' and includes the corrections made by various people in Germany. At the cinema sees the film *Kreutzer Sonate*. Finishes reading Britting's *Kleine Welt am Strom*.

31 March 1937
To Nymphenburg to meet Alverdes in Langen-Müller Verlag. Gives him the typescript of 'Cascando' and a copy of *Echo's Bones*. Alverdes repeats invitation to write an English letter, and expresses his belief that Goebbels will make the right decisions for Germany. Meets the painter Edgard Ende; Beckett recites 'Cascando', talks about his concept of monadic pictures and repeats his assertion that any form of artistic expression must fail. Then on to the Graphisches Kabinett, where Francke shows him his private art collection (which includes paintings by Marc, Müller, Beckmann and Heckel).

1 April 1937
Visits the comedian Karl Valentin with Eichheim. Buys plane ticket back to Croydon. Last tour of the Alte Pinakothek. At Severing's book shop orders Barlach's theatre plays *Der Tote Tag*, *Der Arme Vetter* and *Sündflut*.

2 April 1937
Leaves Germany.

NOTE

1. This chronology was first published in German in *Der Unbekannte Beckett: Samuel Beckett und die deutsche Kultur*, ed. Marion Dieckmann-Fries and Therese Seidel, Frankfurt a. M.: Suhrkamp Verlag, 2005, pp. 34–62. I am grateful to the Suhrkamp Verlag for permission to publish this translation.

REVIEW ESSAYS

RECENT BECKETT CRITICISM IN GERMANY

Franz Michael Maier, *Becketts Melodien. Die Musik und die Idee des Zusammenhangs bei Schopenhauer, Proust und Beckett.* Würzburg: Königshausen & Neumann, 2006. 337pp. €48. ISBN: 978-3-8260-3490-9.

Manfred Milz, *Samuel Beckett und Alberto Giacometti. Das Innere als Oberfläche. Ein ästhetischer Dialog im Zeichen schöpferischer Entzweiungsprozesse (1929–1936).* Würzburg: Königshausen & Neumann, 2006. 303pp. €39.80. ISBN: 3-8260-2990-9.

Carola Veit, *Kraft der Melone. Samuel Beckett im Kino.* Berlin: Verbrecher Verlag, 2009. 114pp. €11. ISBN: 978-3-940426-24-6.

Friedhelm Rathjen, *Beckett. Eine Einführung ins Werk.* Scheeßel: Edition ReJoyce, 2007. 165pp. €17. ISBN: 978-3-00-020690-0.

Friedhelm Rathjen, *weder noch. Aufsätze zu Samuel Beckett.* Scheeßel: Edition ReJoyce, 2005. 166pp. €17. ISBN: 3-00-016654-8.

Since the publication of Jim Knowlson's biography with its now famous chapter on Beckett's diaries, German criticism on the work and life of the writer has been more productive than ever. Beckett's

Journal of Beckett Studies 19.2 (2010): 273–297
Edinburgh University Press
© The editors, *Journal of Beckett Studies*
www.eupjournals.com/jobs

early work, such as *Dream of Fair to middling Women* or *More Pricks Than Kicks*, has received special attention of a new generation of critics. Rapidly translated into German (unlike in France, where one still waits for a French translation of *Dream* or even *Disjecta*, never mind the recently published first volume of Beckett's letters), the publication of these works has contributed significantly to a change in the general perspective on Beckett's work, still very much dependant on philosophical readings, either in the wake of Adorno's famous study of *Endgame* or – more recently – in the light of deconstructive and postmodern approaches to his work. With the discovery of a wealth of hitherto unknown works and documents, new aspects such as Beckett's great interest in painting and music, but also in film, which so obviously mark his early writings, are at the centre of several recent publications.

Franz Michael Maier's study of Beckett's melodies, for instance, whose title seems almost too familiar to Beckett scholars – one thinks immediately of Mary Bryden's volume on *Beckett and Music*, of Anne Henry's and Ulrich Pothast's studies on Schopenhauer's influence on Proust and Beckett, to mention only these – draws an important part of its interest from a long reading of Beckett's *Dream* and its musical structures. Indeed, Maier attempts to show, mainly through a detailed musicologist perspective, how Beckett composed his first novel under the influence of his readings of Schopenhauer and Proust, but also how the mystical experience of music described towards the end of his *Proust* is partially shattered in *Dream*, where Beckett uses the musical metaphor not only to describe, but also to enact his aesthetics of incoherence by putting the overall structure of the novel, the narrator and the protagonist in contradiction. A last part of the book is devoted to a more general overview of the musical images in Beckett's literary production.

The almost uncanny resemblance between the sculptures of Alberto Giacometti such as *Homme qui marche*, and recurring figures of Beckett's fiction (not to mention photographs of the writer himself, such as the ones taken in Tunisia in 1969), as well as the collaboration of the two artists for the 1961 *Godot* production in Paris, have encouraged many readers to search for more thorough common features of their artistic work. In his fairly adventurous study on the aesthetic dialogue between Beckett and Giacometti in the 1930s – that is, before the two men actually met – Manfred

Milz tries to shed light on what he considers to be the common ground of both works: their mostly indirect (in the case of Beckett) or intuitive (Giacometti) reception of Bergson's vitalist philosophy. This reception in turn influenced, mainly through the study of Schopenhauer and Kant, Beckett's conviction of the radical subject–object dichotomy, which permeates his work from the very start. Giacometti's case is more problematic, since Milz himself acknowledges that his work essentially evolves, during this period, through artistic practice, and much less through philosophical readings. Indeed, it is one thing to reconstruct a general "discursive" context for a given period, but quite another thing to analyse the ways in which artists coming from completely different backgrounds cope with similar aesthetic problems. Alas, Milz's study is at once too ambitious in its scope and too sweeping in its statements. Its complicated structure, with a *resumé* at the end, which one is nevertheless supposed to read first, with its rather unmotivated summary of the few personal contacts between the two artists, but also with its too sketchy outline of a common aesthetic context (in fact derived almost exclusively from Beckett's philosophical readings), does not allow the reader to go beyond often vague similarities between two of the major artists of the twentieth century.

Much more modest in scope, but very stimulating is Carola Veit's small study of the films Beckett saw during his stay in Germany in 1936/7. On the basis of Beckett's scant notes (in his German Diaries) on films such as *Mutiny on the Bounty* – Beckett: 'film worse than ever' – Veit succeeds in giving us a lively picture of the young Beckett who, while interested in *avant–garde* film and theory, nevertheless went to see numerous very popular movies.

Let me conclude with two recent volumes by Friedhelm Rathjen, who belongs, like Carola Veit, to the quite rare species of Beckett critics able to combine an excellent and detailed knowledge of the writer's work with a capacity of sharing their discoveries with readers who are not necessarily specialists. Rathjen's introduction to Beckett's work, first published by Junius in 1995 and now re-edited in his own Edition ReJoyce, is still one of the finest sources, at least in German, for a well informed and well written overview of Beckett's work as a whole in only 150 pages. To readers who would like to know more about seemingly secondary (but perhaps rather important!) subjects such as Beckett's bicycles, his translations of Chamfort or his representations of the desert, we recommend to continue their exploration of Beckett's work in the stimulating company of Rathjen, in a collection of essays entitled *weder noch. Aufsätze zu Samuel Beckett* by the same publishing house.

Thomas Hunkeler
DOI: 10.3366/E0309520710000634

GERMAN WANDERINGS: NEW APPROACHES TO BECKETT'S JOURNEY

Der unbekannte Beckett: Samuel Beckett und die deutsche Kultur, eds. Therese Fischer–Seidel and Marion Fries–Dieckmann. Frankfurt a. M.: Suhrkamp, 2005. 358 pp. €11,50. ISBN 3-518-45674-1.

'Obergeschoß still closed.' Samuel Beckett in Berlin 1936/37, eds. Lutz Dittrich, Carola Veit and Ernest Wichner. Berlin: Matthes + Seitz, 2006. 128pp. €24,80. ISBN 978-3-88221-920-3.

Das Raubauge in der Stadt: Beckett liest Hamburg, eds. Michaela Giesing, Gaby Hartel and Carola Veit. Göttingen: Wallstein Verlag, 2007. 220pp. €24,80. ISBN 978-3-8353-0193-1.

Warten auf Godot: Das Absurde und die Geschichte, eds. Denis Thouard and Tim Trzaskalik. Berlin: Matthes + Seitz, 2008. 187pp. €14,80. ISBN 978-3-88221-714-8.

Recent German scholarship on Beckett has been greatly influenced by the publication of James Knowlson's seminal biography *Damned to Fame* (German edition *Samuel Beckett: Eine Biographie*, 2001). Knowlson's extensive discussion of the unpublished *German Diaries* became a source for further investigations of Beckett's journey across Germany in 1936/7, and also an inspiration for the examination of the background to Beckett's artistic development in several fields. The aspiring writer's relation to the fine arts, for instance, has been the subject of further studies contributing to a more comprehensive understanding of Beckett before the *Trilogy* and *Godot*. Thus, the 'biographical turn' within Beckett studies not only focused on biographical facts and data but also opened up a complex interpretation of how Beckett's literary work can be understood and placed within the larger contexts of the respective cultures he came in touch with. Quite naturally, influences from German culture can now be seen as the third major source, after the Anglo–Irish of his childhood and youth and the French culture of his early years as a writer. The 'German Beckett' is, of course, no new phenomenon, as Beckett's work as a director in German theatre is well known and documented while (West) Germany has also been one of the most receptive grounds for Beckett's work since the early 1950s. Yet, a more complex 'German Beckett' has only recently emerged from the renewed scholarly interest ushered in by the 'biographical turn.'

A major step was the interdisciplinary conference 'Samuel Beckett und die deutsche Kultur/Samuel Beckett and German Culture' held in Düsseldorf in March 2004. The volume *Der unbekannte Beckett* (The Unknown Beckett) collects the contributions, carefully edited and introduced by Therese Fischer-Seidel and Marion Fries-Dieckmann. They clearly address Beckett's interest in the arts and 'the role of German culture in the search of identity by the young writer in the 1930s' as the two major fields of consideration with 'the new biographical material' (13). (All translations from the German are my own.) James Knowlson emphasises the importance of Beckett's visits to the family of his uncle William Sinclair in Kassel as the cornerstone for the developing interest in German expressionism, which also motivated Beckett's long journey in 1936/7. Mark Nixon's invaluable chronicle of the journey (34–63) lists all museums and art collections that Beckett visited along his route with extended stays in Hamburg, Berlin and Munich, documenting Beckett's autodidactic but nevertheless methodical studies in art history. Beckett's hunger for art was not only driven by the wish to acquire a visual vocabulary but even more so by his attempts to understand the principles of modern art in relation to problems of representation. 'Beckett discovers the dissonance of subject and object in the early avant-garde,' states art historian Marie Luise Syring with respect to Beckett's interest in expressionist paintings (106), an insight that indeed finds parallels in his prose and dramatic pieces.

By contrast, an examination of what Beckett read from contemporary German literature results in no comparable insight. Mark Nixon uses Beckett's notes in the *Diaries* to check on every book of German literature mentioned there. Not surprisingly, most of them are long forgotten today and belong to a category of fiction tolerated by Nazi censorship while not being explicit propaganda. Nixon sees Beckett's reading of these contemporary German writers as largely fruitless, but argues that it may have helped the young author 'to recognize his own goals more clearly' (152). One striking example is the novel *Necessary Journey* (*Die notwendige Reise*) by Walter Bauer, who was among progressive leftist writers of the late 1920s (and is also mentioned by Knowlson in his biography). Beckett objects to the 'heroic' of Bauer's journey novel in the *Diaries*: 'Journey anyway the wrong figure. How can we travel to that from which one cannot move away. Das notwendige Bleiben (necessary staying put) is more like it' (qtd. on 149). Here, of course, we already see Beckett's sharp eye for existential immobility as contrasted with the heroic figure of a German journey (which, by the way, is also typical of German expressionist drama). This is a fine detail that illustrates a fundamental Beckett motif from *Murphy* to the *Trilogy* and even *Godot*. The significance of Beckett's German journey can be seen as part of a larger development towards a new mode of writing, which Beckett later posited as having taken place in 1946: 'Only then did I begin to write the things I feel.'

Another aspect of the 'German Beckett' is the question as to what extent he learned German and how he made use of that knowledge. This question is, again, not only of biographical interest, since Beckett 'counselled' his German translators in a way that goes beyond the norm for the foreign translation of a literary work. Beckett picked up some German during his first visits to Kassel, and proceeded to study the language, as the vocabulary lists in his 'Exercise Books' show, more seriously in 1934, possibly with the help of a tutor. He then intensified his efforts during the 1936 journey. Marion Fries–Dieckmann surveys these activities with regard to Beckett's attempt to translate his own poem 'Cascando' into German. Beckett's command of German would finally result in his close collaboration with his German translators for aesthetic reasons (221), which are more comprehensively explored in terms of translating principles by Fries–Dieckmann in her study *Beckett und die deutsche Sprache* [see Mark Nixon's review in this issue]. Fries–Dieckmann, however, points out that Beckett was able to motivate his German translators to go against the 'borders of language' and the veil of the German language rather than for a literal translation. Other contributions to *Der unbekannte Beckett* deal with possible influences by German silent film (Gaby Hartel), Beckett's reception of Goethe and Schopenhauer, his work for German TV and, not for the first time, Beckett's encounter with the Bavarian comedian Karl Valentin. Thus, the volume is truly a catalogue featuring nearly all aspects of the now not so unknown 'German Beckett'.

The beautifully designed book *'Obergeschoß still closed.' Samuel Beckett in Berlin 1936/37* was published to accompany a small exhibition at the Berlin Literaturhaus in 2006 focusing on Beckett's six–week visit to Berlin in December 1936 and January 1937. The title – 'Upper floor still closed' – is taken from the *Diaries* and refers to the collection of modern art at the Kronprinzenpalais (a department of the National Gallery) that was not open at the time of Beckett's stay due to the removal of art excluded from the Nazi canon. In the most substantial essay in the volume, Carola Veit shows how systematically Beckett visited the museums in Berlin, and how he documented his favourites from the Italian renaissance and the Dutch baroque as a 'vital relation to paintings' (41). The young writer is shown to have developed into a subjective art historian, who also expanded his knowledge in other areas, such as the collection of Ancient Egypt. There the artful tombs attracted his interest while, outside the museums, in extensive walks, he cultivated the air of a lonesome wanderer and his own pedestrian epistemology, as Gaby Hartel shows. The book contains contemporary photographs of the exhibition halls as Beckett will have seen them, as well as pages from the *Diaries* and documents from museum archives (such as a typescript listing paintings for the defamatory Nazi exhibition on 'Degenerate Art'). Thus, Beckett's German museum journey must be seen in two ways. On the one hand, this was arguably the most intense period of study of the history of art in his life, during which he was able to place artistic achievements according to his own understanding into a kind of mental storage that he could later draw on as a writer.

On the other hand, Beckett not only discovered principles of modern art but also saw how they were rejected and banned by a regime that sought to bring the 'dissonances' under control. Both of these aspects became important in his later work.

The first publication of what was probably Beckett's first dramatic piece looks like a playful conclusion of the 1930s 'German Beckett'. This piece, entitled 'Mittelalterliches Dreieck' (Medieval Triangle), now published in '*Obergeschoß…*,' was written in German on 14 August 1936, before Beckett departed to Hamburg, in one of his exercise books. It displays Beckett's talent to formalise, and render abstract, a traditional subject of literary history along with parody. Ernest Wichner, director of the Berlin Literaturhaus, traces it rightly back to *Orlando Furioso* (97). Yet he overlooks the aspect of parody and self–parody in the stage directions: 'Es dämmert, weil es nicht anders kann.' This translates 'It dawns because it cannot otherwise' and can be compared to the opening line of *Murphy*. For Beckett scholars this is a little gem, as it is the first time this piece has been published. It also shines a light on Beckett's view of romanticism, where he mainly prefers the solitude of the individual to the lost world of knights in armour beneath a shining moon. Beckett was, so to speak, a critical 'German' even before he embarked on his journey to this fascinating, uncanny land of art and aberrance.

Another interdisciplinary conference was held in Hamburg in November 2006, which was part of a larger homage festival 'Beckett in Town,' combining exhibitions, theatre performances and guided tours. Beckett's stay in Hamburg (from 2 October to 3 December 1936) has been well researched. Again, his interest in the fine arts was at the focus of the conference, and four articles in *Das Raubauge in der Stadt. Beckett liest Hamburg* (the conference proceedings) are devoted to this subject. It was only in Hamburg that Beckett was able to visit artists in their studios and find out about their situation in relation to Nazi policies on modern art. Yet it was not only his encounters with painters such as Karl Ballmer and Willem Grimm, but also the already banned book on modern German art, *Die Kunst der letzten dreißig Jahre* (Art of the Last Thirty Years, 1935) by art historian Max Sauerlandt and his acquaintance with the Jewish collector Rosa Schapire that gave Beckett a profound introduction and first–hand insights that he would only rarely be able to acquire that way on his journey. Maike Bruhns explains the context of Beckett's encounters with Hamburg artists in her short history of the 'Hamburgische Sezession', an association of *avant-garde* artists founded in 1919. Carola Veit analyses Beckett's notes in the *Diaries* based on his visit to the studios of Ballmer, Grimm and Karl Kluth, in whose paintings he observed 'a very strong Munch influence' (qtd. on 116). Beckett's visits to the collections of the Hamburger Kunsthalle are the basis for Matthias Mühling's argument that Beckett was attracted, across the centuries, by works of 'auratic stillness of things and bodies' (127). Franz Michael Maier reconstructs Beckett's visit to the home of Rosa Schapire, where a discussion about Schapire's portrait by Karl Schmidt-Rottluff (1919) turned out to be awkward for the young writer. And yet, Maier is able to show how such misunderstandings went into the *Diaries* as part of a quest for aesthetic principles. In this case, the product was Beckett's examination of 'the art that is a prayer' (quoted p. 133). Drawing a conclusion from these contributions on Beckett and the fine arts in Hamburg, one also recognises the *Diaries* as a sketchbook of theory of modern art.

A rather unusual academic approach is taken by Eckart Voigts-Virchow, who shows how Beckett and his work have been appropriated by contemporary popular culture with amateurish stagings on YouTube or 'corpsed' in a parody of *Nacht und Träume* by the German late-night comedian Harald Schmidt. Voigts-Virchow catalogues anything and everything that is excluded from serious academic concerns and quotes the Irish critic Patrick Lonergan, who, with regard to a less intimidating Beckett, called for an approach to his writing 'in terms of what it says about us, rather than what it reveals about Beckett' (qtd. on 209). This makes for a great counterpoint and coda to a conference whose papers were influenced by the 'biographical turn' and close readings of fragments from the *Diaries*.

A small collection of new essays on *Godot* has been translated from French, and only in Germany have they been compiled as a book so far. It is perhaps the most sensational recent book about Beckett's most famous play, as it offers no less than an entirely new interpretation. Theatre historian Valentin Temkine, whose personal history with the play begins with the Paris world *première* in 1953, interprets the characters Vladimir and Estragon as Jewish refugees from Paris on their way to Italy in 1943. Pozzo is a landowner and enemy of the Résistance, while Godot is the secret Résistance contact who will guide the refugees across the border at night. Temkine published his very straightforward interpretation for the first time in the journal *UBU* in April 2002 under the title 'Le puzzle réconstitué ou Beckett revisité' (republished at the end of the book). Temkine's initial impulse, as he states in the opening interview conducted by his grandson Pierre Temkine (14), was to find an explanation as to why Didi and Gogo were not allowed to climb the Eiffel tower. In fact, there was an order under German occupation that excluded Jews from accessing certain public buildings. Valentin Temkine develops a coherent interpretation based on Jewish refugees in a concrete historical situation by way of further evidence in Beckett's text, reconstructing the biographical background of the protagonists and some geographical detail. This interpretation is very convincing and, of course, raises the question whether the play has been the subject of fifty years of 'blind' or mis-reception.

Co-editor Denis Thouaurd argues that metaphysical interpretations of *Godot* obliterated its documentary and historical core from the very beginning. Beckett did not object, as he knew that the play was strong enough to stand against all competing and also contradictory interpretations (p. 131). The point now, however, is that the discovery of the historical layer and Temkine's interpretation saves the play, long overdue, from 'being mummified as a classic of the absurd' (p. 132). The potential of this new reception is summed up as follows: 'The human beings in *Waiting for Godot* are universal in their humanity because they were made into these human beings through a distinct and unique historical experience' (132).

The book was reviewed in German newspapers as a groundbreaking new reading of *Godot* and has already made an impact on German theatre. The first production that largely followed Temkine's interpretation premiered in Stendal in November 2009. Director Hannes Hametner emphasised the plight of refugees desperately needing to identify their unknown contact by means of a stage design that was slightly reminiscent of France in the early 1940s. Furthermore, the casting of Didi and Gogo with elderly actors, as suggested by Temkine for the 'real' biographies, supported the general idea. This staging of *Godot* was evidence of how compelling Temkine's interpretation can be, but also left the audience with new questions unanswered. Why would refugees of 1943 talk about whispering dead bodies (second act) as if from a post-Holocaust perspective? Not that Temkine is inconsistent, but his interpretation is certainly not comprehensive enough to explain questions that go beyond the correctly identified historical layer in *Godot*.

The collection by the Temkines can also be seen in the wake of the 'biographical turn', but has little to do with Knowlson's biography and the *German Diaries*. Rather, one should now look for further examination of how Beckett's immediate post-war experience (for example in Saint Lô) went into *Godot* along with the fate of Paris Jews whose journey was really terminated in terrifying silence.

Thomas Irmer
DOI: 10.3366/E0309520710000646

BECKETT AND THE GERMAN LANGUAGE

Marion Fries-Dieckmann, *Samuel Beckett und die deutsche Sprache; Eine Untersuchung der deutschen Übersetzungen des dramatischen Werks*. Trier: Wissenschaftlicher Verlag Trier, 2007. 236pp. €24,50. ISBN: 978-3-88476-879-2.

Marion Fries-Dieckmann's *Samuel Beckett und die deutsche Sprache* is the first sustained examination of the role the German language played in Beckett's work, aesthetics, and, more importantly, his understanding of the translation process. Both in scope and depth this book is impressive; it covers Beckett's own command of and attitude to the German language, his involvement in the German translations of his work by Elmar (and Erika) Tophoven, and the way that his understanding of the German language contributed to his dramatic work. At the same time it touches upon the way that Beckett generally viewed the art of translation, and the way in which his translation practice anticipated a paradigm shift in translation theory. Thus Beckett's view of the translation process predates a shift in thinking ushered in by poststructuralist theories of the text, which moved from technical, linguistic translations to a textual 'transposition' that admits other criteria, such as intended readers or cultural contexts. In the process, Fries-Dieckmann convincingly shows how the complexities of translation, revolving around issues such as 'self', 'other', 'difference', 'alienation' and 'appropriation' resonate with topics inherent to Beckett's work.

The initial focus of this book is on Beckett's critique of language *per se*, charting his early comments on the inadequacies of literature *vis-à vis* the visual arts, and his interest in language criticism, such as the one established by Fritz Mauthner. The following chapter investigates, in the first instance, Beckett's translations of other authors in the 1930s and beyond, before turning to an overview of his translations of his own work. As Fries-Dieckmann points out, Beckett's first self-translation was from English to German (antedating Beckett's move to writing in French), and her insightful discussion of his translation of the poem 'Cascando' into German reveals an early attempt to inscribe the change of language in the translation itself. The following chapter hones in on Beckett's specific work on the German translations undertaken by Elmar Tophoven, and his relationship with his German publishers the Suhrkamp Verlag.

The second half of the study investigates the way in which the German translations transpose the source texts. Fries-Dieckmann here concentrates on Beckett's drama in practical case studies, from *Godot* to *Ohio Impromptu*. Throughout this book, the emphasis is on *dramatic language*, that it so say the way in which Beckett shaped his translations toward a more 'visual language' [*bildliche Sprache*]. This discussion is extremely interesting; not only does Fries-Dieckmann examine the evolution of Beckett's translation practice across different dramatic texts, she also highlights the way in which these theatrical texts are rendered more visual and dramatic, by drawing on what Beckett called the 'plastic' quality of the German language. This is substantiated by Beckett's own work as a director in Germany and underlines the view, first proposed by James Knowlson, that Beckett's German texts are the most authoritative. Such an evaluation is further strengthened by the fact that changes made during Beckett's directorial work were incorporated in subsequent publications. As such the publication of the drama by Suhrkamp Verlag represents the only instance where Beckett's textual, and more importantly, 'theatrical' changes to the texts were taken into account. Beckett trusted one man more than any other when it came to his German texts – Elmar Tophoven. Tophoven of course has published articles detailing his work with Beckett, but the additional value of this study is that the author has consulted the Tophovens' archive in order to chart the minute process of translating Beckett's work.

On the whole, *Samuel Beckett und die deutsche Sprache* shows Beckett's active role in the translations of his work into German, and the way this work helped to shape his entire creative enterprise. That is to say, and this was a genuine revelation to me, Beckett's work on the German translations with the Tophovens more often than not predates the self-translation between French and English (which is usually the scrutiny of Beckett scholarship). Thus the German context informs not only Beckett's self-translations, but undoubtedly also his subsequent creative writing. Moreover, and this is equally interesting, Beckett also consulted draft material when translating, which introduces a complexity of cultural and linguistic transposition.

Following on from work done on Beckett and translation, such as Friedman, Rossmann and Sherzer's collection of 1987 and Brian T. Fitch's volume of 1988, this is the first substantial treatment of Beckett's attitudes toward language, translation, and self-translation in a long time, and the reader will find much of interest here.

Mark Nixon
DOI: 10.3366/E0309520710000658

Isabelle Ost, *Samuel Beckett et Gilles Deleuze: Cartographie de deux parcours d'écriture*, Bruxelles: Publications des facultés universitaires Saint-Louis, 2008. 444pp. €59,00. ISBN: 2-8028-0182-5.

Samuel Beckett and Gilles Deleuze inhabited the same city, Paris, for some five decades, sharing the same publisher, Jérôme Lindon of Editions de Minuit. Both enjoyed a high level of prominence during that period. Deleuze's collaboration with Félix Guattari came to the fore around the time of the May 1968 uprisings, resulting, over the next twelve years, in the two paradigm-shifting volumes of *Capitalisme et Schizophrénie*. During those years, Beckett was awarded the Nobel Prize for Literature (1969), and directed some high-profile productions of his plays. Nevertheless, there was no direct contact between the two writers, and during his conversations with the young André Bernold, some five decades his junior, Beckett took the opportunity of finding out more about Deleuze. Bernold, a student of both Deleuze and Derrida, answered Beckett's questions on Deleuze's teaching style and tone of voice by recounting how Deleuze would set out his concepts like jewels, selecting their most beautiful facet and laying them out as if on an immaculate table cloth. When Beckett asked him what kind of people these philosophers were, Bernold said that both Deleuze and Derrida were distinguished by their courtesy, patience, and generosity: 'au fond, ils étaient nobles [...]. Beckett fut satisfait de la réponse' [They were essentially noble [...]. Beckett was satisfied with this reply].[1]

Underlying Beckett's questions about the nature of direct communication with philosophers is an implied assumption that there is no automatic affinity between philosophical and literary activity. Indeed, this is a question which lies at the heart of Isabelle Ost's sustained investigation, fruit of her doctoral thesis on Beckett and Deleuze. While Beckett disavowed his own credentials as a philosopher and creator of thought, Deleuze's thought is one which is deeply permeated with artistic and literary insights. Hence, Ost finds it legitimate to explore the extent to which Beckett is indeed a philosopher in the Deleuzian sense. Both Beckett and Deleuze, she points out, refuse to be confined within given parameters; both work *between* ['entre'] literary, social, political and philosophical fields; both are deeply suspicious of systems of representation; both reject notions of mastery, in order to embrace the minor, the provisional.

This struggle draws both writers, Ost argues, into a twin process – (Ost calls it 'paradoxical', but it might simply be thought of as double) – of emptying and generating. In subtracting, purifying, lessening, there is also a movement not so much towards extinction as towards intensification. It is notable, in fact, that Deleuze became interested in the process of 'épuration' [purifying], by means of which an artist's or writer's late style may sometimes exhibit an increasing sobriety or brevity. Beckett's late writing may exemplify this process, as may also Deleuze's commentary upon it, especially in his careful, distilled commentary on Beckett's television plays. Entitled *L'Epuisé*, it was one of his last works before his suicide in 1995.

Ost points out that the anti-representational dynamic must be also be tracked in relation to the evacuated subject, which is in constant mutation, along with a temporal and spatial flux which operates in multiple directions. Adopting the Deleuzo-Guattarian concept of 'lines of flight', Ost divides her analysis along five key points, occupying the five chapters of the book. She attributes the establishment of these five points to Beckett's late text *Worstward Ho*. (Disconcertingly, this text only occasionally receives its correct title in the analysis, appearing variously as *Wortward Ho*, *Wortsward Ho*, and even *Wotsward Ho*.) Two of these five elements relate to place – the wider environment against which 'quelque chose', some body or thing, is made manifest. These two elements are empty space ['le vide'] and half-shadow ['la pénombre'], and they begin and end the analysis (chapters one and five). Between these bookends feature three shadowy elements which are located by Ost in *Worstward Ho*: the 'moi', the first-person pronoun (the second chapter); the pair of characters, the couple (the third chapter); the head, figure of thought (fourth chapter). Within the grey emptiness covered by the first and last chapters, the three intervening chapters, taken together, constitute subjectivity. As Ost memorably puts it: 'Il faut trois ombres, chez Beckett, pour dire un sujet' [In Beckett, you need three shadows to speak of a subject].

There is much rewarding discussion within each of the chapters of this substantial book, of which this review can give only a flavour. Chapter 1 examines the *Trois Dialogues* in terms of Beckett's resistance to the notion of a 'work of art', posing the alternative model of art as a 'non-sens', a process which eschews the creation of meaning. Ost presents this wedding to failure as one of the founding insights which was to underlie Beckett's literary endeavours. Picking up Deleuze's analysis, in *L'Epuisé*, of the exhaustion of possibilities found in Beckett's work, Ost pores around the many workings of Beckett's 'machinerie du vide' (102), concluding that its many fluxes and refluxes always deter the empty space from becoming nothingness ['néant']. In Chapter 2, Ost cites Badiou's description of that process of reduction which still delivers up a singular characteristic or feature. In the case of *Worstward Ho* or *Mal vu mal dit*, this could be the bowed back of the old woman, a persistent vestige. The shadow becomes the particle of minimal existence, always threatened with further fragmentation.

Where, amongst all this, asks Ost, may the voice, the someone, be located? Not in the taboo first person, it seems. She recruits *Compagnie* to demonstrate the triadic subject made up of the one who listens, the voice addressed to the listener, and the third person who belies the solitude professed in the last word of that text. Somewhere among these negotiations is the trace of life, whatever persists when everything else has been taken away. What in my view constitutes the most compelling routepath between Deleuze and Beckett – the 'minoration' of language and subjectivity – is explored by Ost in her penultimate chapter, where she links the notion with Beckett's bilingualism, his nomadic travelling between languages. Time and space – as the final chapter explores – also participate in this shuttling between two frontiers. At the close of Ost's study, Beckettian subjectivity remains under the Deleuzian sign of permanent 'becoming': on a trajectory to zero, but never eradicated.

As its title promises, Ost's study provides a 'cartography', a method of mapping and journeying among the rhizomatic spaces of Beckett and Deleuze. It provides a good account of scholarship in French on the Beckett/Deleuze conjunction – (one would not expect a full account of existing Anglo–American scholarship on the pairing) – and it has the merit of ranging across most of Beckett's literary output rather than restricting itself to prose, or drama. In doing so, it carefully draws out between literature and philosophy, as Beckett and Deleuze practised them, 'un dehors et un dedans réciproques' [a reciprocal outside and inside] (403), and is to be recommended for that.

Mary Bryden
DOI: 10.3366/E030952071000066X

NOTE

1. Bernold, André (1992), *L'Amitié de Beckett*, Paris: Hermann, 86.

GODOT AND HIS SHADOW

Antoni Libera, *Godot I Jego Cien*, Krakow: Wydawnictwo Znak, 2009. 414pp. 36.90 zlotys. ISBN 978-83-240-1094-3.

In this 414-page memoir-cum-intellectual autobiography, Antoni Libera offers a lively account (in Polish) of his early years as a Beckett acolyte, from the time he saw *Godot* as an 8-year-old on the Warsaw stage to the time of his first meeting with Beckett in Paris at the age of 29.

Recalling the drabness of his youth in the hopeless atmosphere of early post-war Poland, Libera sets the stage for his fateful encounters with Beckett (first through his works, then in person), who served as an inspirational beacon in his professional and personal life. It was in autumn of 1957, during the first year of the post-Stalinist thaw, that the 8-year-old first heard the expression 'waiting for Godot', which had become a leitmotif of the frustrations felt by many, in light of the changes promised by Gomulka's 'reformed' Communist government. As it happened, *Godot* had been playing to packed houses (in Polish) in Warsaw's Contemporary Theatre for ten months before his parents were able to secure tickets. This was to be Libera's startling initiation to 'adult' theatre.

Eleven years later, Libera came upon a collection of *Dialog* issues, a journal devoted to contemporary drama, first published in 1956. This was to be the key turning point in the 19-year-old's intellectual development; it was in *Dialog* that he was able to read (albeit in Polish) Beckett's major theatrical works for the first time. Every piece he read in these issues led to an increasingly deeper sense of self-understanding. Henry's inventive fabulations in the face of the menacing void (in *Embers*) fascinated him; Krapp's working his way into the core of his failed existence, transforming it into exquisitely musical prosody, filled him with admiration; while *Endgame*'s seemingly mordant catastrophism filled him with awe. All of these incantatory works struck the young Libera to the quick, stirring up disturbing existential intuitions and recollections going back to his early childhood, resulting in the dual realisation that a) the oppressiveness confronting him (and Beckett's characters as well) lay both without and within individual consciousnesss;

and b) that verbal articulation–even if seemingly addressed to oneself alone–was the most expedient means to transform the stranglehold of this interdependent oppressiveness into a coherent expression. Or, when words failed, chess, which he learned as a young boy, might also provide him with the tools with which to confront life's riddled complexities. Everything, however, seemed to be aleatory, and thus subject to grievous doubts. Everything in *Endgame* put everything in question, including itself. And yet it all seemed to amount to something, and Libera was increasingly drawn into the world of Samuel Beckett.

Just two months after Beckett's Nobel Prize award in October 1969, Libera was already staging *Endgame* in a Warsaw students' production. In the meantime, he'd been reading as much of Beckett's prose works as he could lay his hands on (once having to 'save' Beckett from the strict confines of Warsaw's Military Library by sneaking the only available copy of *Stories and Texts for Nothing* in Polish translation out of its forced reclusion), which only heightened the sensation of somehow sharing common ground with the fundamental sounds of Beckett's sharply focussed vision. His invitation to observe Roger Blin's May 1970 Warsaw rehearsals of *Fin de Partie* then served to ground this conviction as an article of faith.

With his chance discovery in September 1970 of *Lessness* (in the Polish review, *Tworzosc*) on his first journey beyond the iron curtain, Libera began to fathom the extent to which Beckett's writings were resonant with his own existential and metaphysical questionings. Struck by the contrasts between the twisted ideological conceits that prevailed in the world from which he had momentarily emerged, and the dazzling display of the fruits of freedom in the West, he found himself, one day, standing before Stockholm's Royal Academy building, just one year after Beckett's Nobel Prize. Here, in an epiphanic moment, Libera intrinsically seemed to sense that the author of *Godot* epitomised the parting of the ways, between the ideological reactions of writers such as Gombrowicz or Milosz to the perceived threat of the disintegration of Western European civilisation, and a more introspective questioning of the dilemma.

From this point on, midway in his intellectual autobiography, Libera reconstructs the intricacies of his progressive immersion in Beckett's polymorphic world. Systematically questioning the various attempts already made to crack the Beckett code, he makes a strong case for sticking to (and with) the Beckett text as the only viable means of getting to the core of his world. But how to do this from behind the Iron Curtain, with state censorship ready to clamp down on the first hints of Western, decadent, bourgeois experimentation? And with a severely limited number of readers having sufficient profiency in English or French? The first thing to do was to find means to publish all of Beckett's works, beyond *Godot* and *Endgame* in Polish translation. Second, a selection of critical analyses by established scholars abroad also had to be made available to Polish readers. Third, it was imperative to bring all of Beckett's dramatic work to the Polish stage. (For an overview of this multifaceted project, see my 'Sam w Polsce/Sam in Poland' review essay, *JOBS* nos. 11&12, 1989; also 'Beckett's Continuing Presence in Poland,' *JOBS*, vol.17, nos. 1&2, 2008.)

In the meantime, while actively engaged in the nascent Solidarity movement, Libera was invited to Berlin in mid-November 1976 to see the Schiller Theatre productions of *Footfalls* and *That Time*, which Beckett had just directed. Since Libera was in the process of translating these works, Beckett agreed that it would be a good thing for him to see them in the dramatic shapes and movements that he, Beckett, had given them. However, Libera was prevented by the authorities from leaving Warsaw, raising Beckett's political consciousness as to the events that were dramatically unfolding in Poland (see James Knowlson's *Damned to Fame*, Simon & Schuster, pp. 563–65).

Ten months later, in September 1977, Libera managed to pass through the maze of Kafkaesque measures that had kept him from exiting Poland for the past seven years. Arriving in New York for three months' research, he was admittedly surprised by the scope of actvities surrounding Beckett's work everywhere he turned. His meetings with Alan Schneider and David Warrilow strengthened his own belief in the redemptive powers of theatre–and in particular, of Beckett's inquisitive, dramatic probes, centred on the fundamental issue of man's universal condition and fate.

Returning to Europe in late December 1977, Libera decided to stop over in London. The impressions he had gathered during his New York stay were too vivid to risk being snuffed out by a sudden transitionless return to Warsaw's hermetic and suffocating clime. His reflections on the conceptual transformations that were brewing within him as a result of his three months spent abroad provide the raw material for his longest (and perhaps most incisive) chapter, 'Speech, Agape [in the theological sense], Thought,' devoted to a detailed analysis of *That Time*, the most striking example of Beckett's parabolic theatre. Its spiral, three-part construction, Libera argues, touches on the insufficiencies of our Western anthro/mythopoetic consciousness, as an endlessly repeated cycle of hyperbolic articulations and dispelled hypotheses.

From here on, Libera's narrative takes on an intensity which reaches a climax (four chapters later) with his meeting Beckett in Paris for the first time, on 5 January 1978, at the Café de France of the PLM Hotel. With his penultimate chapter, titled 'Enfin!' (Beckett's word of greeting to Libera, thus commemorating their several failed attempts to meet before this moment), Libera's memoir comes full circle, as he echoes his initiatory experience of Beckett's theatre with the 1957 performance of *Godot* in Warsaw, which he saw at the tender age of $8\frac{1}{2}$. To which Beckett replied, with a broad smile: 'You mean they let you in? That isn't a play for children.' Having thus broken the proverbial ice, Libera confided to Beckett the extraordinary impact of Beckett's work on his own personal development from that moment on.

Back in London shortly after his meeting with Beckett, Libera (in his 'Epilog on the Thames') reflects on the transformational effect it had on him, as if he were about to enter a new phase, ready to confront fate with renewed vigour. In the meantime, however, he was still struggling with inner ghosts (triggered by his private viewing – arranged thanks to Beckett – of the recently filmed *Ghost Trio*, *…but the clouds…*, and *Not I* in the BBC TV studios): who/what was it within him that was still stirring, after all these years, with increasing urgency, crying out for recognition? Music had failed him (he thought), love had deceived him; not yet 30, Libera felt dispossessed of a discernible sense of self, as something or someone more or other than the void within. Like so many of Beckett's characters, he had been reaching out for words that could somehow reinscribe a sense of self in spite of himself. Now, with the impressions that meeting Beckett had imprinted upon his deepest level of consciousness, he felt armed with the wherewithal that would perhaps allow him to accede to self-possession.

It was time, now, to act. Opening his travel-diary, he saw in it the makings of a possible breakthrough, a means to give him voice, *his* voice, that could speak of him, indeed that could express, and thus give form, to the formlessness that had been fermenting inside him all this time.

Charles Krance
DOI: 10.3366/E0309520710000671

UNKNOWN IN SIX CONTINENTS

Other Edens: the life and work of Brian Coffey, edited by Benjamin Keatinge and Aengus Woods. Dublin: Irish Academic Press, 2009. 304pp. £40/€39,95). ISBN 978-0-7165-2910-1.

Here is what must be – even in the absence of such persuasive advocates as Alex Davis, Dónal Moriarty and Stan Smith – the most varied and sustained homage ever paid to Brian Coffey (1905–95), who liked to think of himself as, and for a long time actually was, 'unknown in six continents', as Augustus Young recalls (13). Where Coffey has been known, more often than not in the eyes of the Irish themselves, it has been *inter pares*, as it were, in the company of the so-called 'Irish Modernists': Thomas MacGreevy, Denis Devlin, George Reavey and, of course, Samuel Beckett. In a 1996 essay J. C. C. (James) Mays wondered whether 'the association of his name with that of Beckett and Devlin, in Ireland, has done him much good'. It has, however, certainly kept Coffey's name alive, the poet having spent most of a long life out of Ireland, in Paris, St Louis, London, and latterly Southampton. In a ground-breaking 1974 essay by Stan Smith, Coffey was seen as an example of 'vagrancy' and of 'exile [...] as an ontological given'. But one of this book's editors (Keatinge) quotes Coffey in a 1959 letter to MacGreevy (reproduced in photographic facsimile, alongside numerous splendid photographs) as 'still quite unreconciled to the role of foreigner', and still believing that 'We could have been

more "useful" at home', thoughts prompted in part by hearing of
the death of Devlin in New York. Coffey was, on this evidence
at least, less inured than Beckett to being 'always elsewhere',
even if the idea of 'home' was always kept in tension with his
notions of 'otherness'. But *Other Edens* remains an apt title for this
admirably ambitious book, however much it may contain hells and
purgatories closer and more familiar.

So full and diverse is this collection (which began life in a
centenary symposium at TCD) that it would be virtually impossible
in the short space of a review to pay tribute to its contributors
in anything like an adequate manner: there are nineteen of them,
over 'twenty-one 'chapters', with a very full bibliography added
for even better measure, and itself a stimulus to further scholarship,
courtesy of Aengus Woods. Several of the essays – notably those by
James Matthew Wilson, Harry Gilonis, Waclaw Grzybowski and
Andrew Goodspeed – are extremely challenging in their responses
to a poet who has (not unnaturally perhaps) tended to be seen
as 'difficult'. Even though these writers expertly dismantle the
relevant issues, and end up justifying their understandably strong
emphasis on how lucid Coffey really is, one needs to know some of
Coffey's most demanding work – *Advent* (1974 and 1982) and *Death
of Hektor* (1979 and 1982) in particular – very well indeed to feel that
they might soon become more common currency than has thus far
been the case. But even if Coffey still looks, after all their efforts,
too 'writerly' to be easily read, they certainly cannot be accused
of having failed to put him in a position from which he can be
approached and brought closer.

For Coffey as a living person one naturally turns to the four
personal memoirs here – by Augustus Young, Billy Mills, Michael
Smith and the poet's son, John Coffey – which convey a most
attractive personality, a likeable and modest man, reassuringly
ordinary in spite of possessing a quite formidable intellect. These
memoirs are reinforced by a very welcome study of 'a friendship
of lasting importance' with George Reavey as fully documented
by Sandra O'Connell, which is especially compelling (58–9) in its
account of how Reavey wrote (in English) a sequence of twenty-
eight poems (*Frailties* or *The Frailty of Love*) in late 1932, 'after
the death of his French lover Andrée Conte'. Fourteen of these
(in Pierre Charnay's translation) became *Signes d'Adieu*, alongside

Beckett's *Echo's Bones and Other Precipitates* and Coffey's *Image at the Cinema*, in the first tranche of titles from Reavey's new Europa Poets initiative in 1935, and (as Reavey much later recalled) 'Beckett admired them very much'; they are, apparently, still unpublished in English, a situation which ought surely to be remedied.

On Coffey as published there could be no more expert guide than Thomas Dillon Renshaw, who contributes here two important chapters in the modern discipline of 'history of the book', which are just the kind of tribute an 'unknown' figure ought to receive. Geoffrey Squires is equally exact in what looks like a rather dry 'note on prosody', but which puts 'Eight Lines of Coffey' under a very powerful microscope, from which Coffey, rather refreshingly, does not always emerge unscathed. Squires very honestly admits to finding the eighth and final section of *Advent* 'unconvincing' (45), and very bravely proposes that when Coffey deals with 'the big themes of love, art and religion' he is not particularly successful (43). In person Coffey comes across as engaging and deeply committed, but there are certainly times when the poetry is, as Beckett memorably said (and as remembered here by Renshaw; 70), 'another pair of sleeves'. Less often remembered in this connection, it must be said, is how in the same letter (to MacGreevy; 9/1/[1936]) Beckett found Coffey's humour a leavening factor in his intensity, and concluded 'Still there is far more there than in Devlin, I think'. These are of course judgments of both the man and his poems in the mid-1930s, long before Coffey had found his most appealing voice in 'Missouri Sequence' (1962), 'Mindful of You' and 'Answering Mindful' (also 1962) and 'For What For Whom Unwanted' (1977). The two editors devote their own excellent essays to these, all of which are important ports of call in Coffey's long and slow return to poetry, which throughout the 1930s and 1940s had to take second place to philosophy and teaching, his 'first period' having effectively come to an end with the collection *Third Person*, published by George Reavey's Europa Press (one of its last hurrahs, from its London quarters) in 1938. *Third Person* is the subject of an essay by Maria Johnston which treats the poems on the basis of her collaborative project with the young Irish composer Scott McLaughlin.

The fourteenth and last poem in *Third Person* ('One Way') is as demanding as any in the collection, but of special interest as a kind of footnote to the Murphy/Mr Endon situation in Beckett's novel. Indeed, with Mr Endon in mind, it seems impossible not to think that there are at least two lines in the much later sequence 'Daybreak' which hark back to that *Murphy* moment, when Coffey describes a 'white radiance' which 'makes him unseen by her in his eyes close to him/O pure indifference of inattention' (quoted from poem '33' in the fourth number of *The Lace Curtain*, Summer, 1971). But in 'inattention' some of the stuttering of *Third Person* has interestingly diminished, and Aengus Woods, in his essay on 'the metaphysics of love', explores another important change in the later work, with Coffey moving on from an emphasis on the 'reciprocal dynamics' between the lover and the loved one, a dualism which in Coffey is never merely personal (however firmly it may have been grounded in a happy marriage) but always cerebral and philosophical, the product of prolonged mediation on St Thomas Aquinas, Jacques Maritain and other much less well–known philosophers. Woods demonstrates with great skill how Coffey's similarly prolonged exposure to Mallarmé moved his 'dynamics' in the direction of 'the absolute singularity and unknowability of the other' (145).

For 'reciprocal dynamics' in the literary sphere, however, it would be hard to match Beckett and Coffey in the years before the war, and especially in Paris between 1936 and 1938. It was Coffey who encouraged Beckett's interest in Geulincx, who helped him with the George Routledge proofs of *Murphy* in the Hôpital Broussas, who put some distance between him and Peggy Guggenheim, and who was given in return the title for his *Third Person* collection. In due course he was also given the six notebooks towards *Murphy* (which are of course *not*, as implied on page 96, at Reading – would they were!). A clearer understanding of Coffey's presence in, or absence from, the writing of *Murphy* will of course have to wait, who knows how long, for those very notebooks to emerge from the hugger–mugger in which they have been immured for decades by their present owner. But at least in the interim we can be grateful for the retrieval of a text written by Coffey in Paris in March 1938, the month in which *Murphy* was published, which has itself not seen the light of day for more than seventy years. 'I cannot', writes Coffey, 'condense the meaning to an attar of pain' (87); and I cannot myself even begin to convey what an extraordinary performance this previously unpublished review is from every point of view. It has every bit of the 'living ginger' that W B Yeats found in his brother Jack's novel *The Charmed Life*, also published by George Routledge & Co. early in 1938, and it will keep Beckett commentators on *Murphy* busy puzzling out its implications for a good while to come. From *The Letters of Samuel Beckett 1929–1940* we learn that Coffey's review was sent to *Ireland Today* (613), a journal which was (like so many of those with which Beckett had any dealings with before the war) on its last legs. It seems safe to suppose (as James Mays does, in his most helpful introductory essay) that the review never could in fact have enjoyed much chance of appearing anywhere, given its remarkable twists and turns, with Coffey in full flow, freer perhaps than he ever was on his own behalf.

There is a priceless moment in this review where Coffey very deftly disposes of an analogy in what must presumably be a riposte to Peggy Guggenheim (later, in 1945, to make much of the Beckett =Oblomov connection in *Out Of This Century*): 'Murphy, who wants indifference, is not Oblomov' (89). The word 'wants' is very carefully chosen, conveying both a desire and a lack, as Coffey's poetry often does; and it embodies a much tougher approach than Peggy Guggenheim could have countenanced, however clearly Beckett saw himself in the Goncharov novel under her influence (see the *Letters*, 590–92, to MacGreevy and to Reavey). Perhaps Beckett himself might have found 'the best review [*Murphy*] never had' (Mays on 93) more than he could easily cope with, and in some ways alien to his own way of thinking, though his gift of the notebooks was characteristically generous. No doubt 'much good' will one day come from all this, but what most matters overall here is that *Other Edens* can do nothing but good for the better understanding of Brian Coffey. Congratulations to all concerned or, in the Latin to which the poet was so often drawn, *Plaudite omnes*.

John Pilling
DOI: 10.3366/E0309520710000683

PRODUCTION REVIEWS

REVIEW OF *ENDGAME*, DIRECTED BY SIMON MCBURNEY

Endgame, directed by Simon McBurney, at The Duchess Theatre, London. Cast: Simon McBurney as Clov, Mark Rylance as Hamm, Miriam Margolyes as Nell, Tom Hickey as Nagg, Complicite Theatre Company, 2 October–5 December 2009

In the programme accompanying Complicite's first Beckett production, Simon McBurney (the company's founder, director of this performance, and here also playing Clov) responds to questions about *Endgame*'s radical originality when first staged in 1958. Discussing the play's impact on subsequent theatre he points out that 'The shock of a curtain going up and there being nothing on stage is not the same anymore.' Complicite's productions themselves have a reputation for originality. Their workshop approach to rehearsal involves all sorts of exercises, games and experiments related to particular elements of a play, from broad underlying themes to fragments of text, in an attempt to find and mine a work's unexplored possibilities. For a number of theatregoers anticipation is high for this meeting of old and new innovators.

The curtain rises on Hamm centre stage in the chair with his accursed progenitors' ashbins placed stage left, Clov's door stage

Journal of Beckett Studies 19.2 (2010): 298–305
Edinburgh University Press
© The editors, *Journal of Beckett Studies*
www.eupjournals.com/jobs

right. The atmosphere of the ominous smoke-filled shelter-bunker is very impressive as the lights go up on a suitably frayed and stark set by Tim Hatley. The room seems to fade into further background at its edges through the smoke and shadings of darker greys to black. Less hermetically sealed from the world than some kind of cancerous outcrop of it, the space almost breathes, with the fetid smoke, final breaths.

Most immediately striking about Clov when he enters to remove the sheets is how physically broad McBurney is playing in a shabby, oversized vest. Perhaps it is the director's reputation for the physicality of his theatre, but this subjugated subject looks like he could probably pick up and throw his much leaner autocratic master out of one of those back windows if he chose. McBurney tempers this latent power by performing hunched and shuffling throughout, whereas Clov's various verbal hesitations are often accompanied by a half-hearted shambling in one direction then another. By turns he also sometimes moves with focused, determined speed, scuttling about along straight lines like one of Beckett's rats. This doubled style is most pointed in the opening mime, during which, as the stage directions minimally have it, 'He gets down' from the ladder. After hustling up the ladder enunciating his pronounced limp, McBurney manoeuvres this bad leg to allow him to slide back down to the ground in a second. He repeats this each time he uses the ladder, labouring up before sliding down. This is a nice touch that bears out the freedom within constraint frequently described as permitted by, or sealed in to, Beckett's taut stage directions (this is mentioned in the after show talk and in the program). A similar comic flourish is given to Clov's coming and going through the door. The door swings into and out of the room with a quick squeak, before it comes to rest flush with the false wall. Clov thrusts the door when leaving the stage and it swings to let him through, holds half a second fully open, then swings back again to open onto the stage as fully as if it had been pushed from offstage, and Clov re-enters while it is fully open in this opposite direction. Each time he uses the door he does so in this way, and along with a few other emphases of rhythmic slapstick timing manages to bring out some original comedy from the play's crevices of repetition and entropy.

Mark Rylance as Hamm revels in the role as a madman of many qualities. British theatre's man of the moment, Rylance won Best Actor at the Evening Standard Theatre Awards 2009 and at the Laurence Olivier Awards 2010 for his role as Jonny Byron in *Jerusalem*, and comes to Hamm between that original performance and its reprisal at the Apollo Theatre. Similarly to his co-star, Rylance wants to dig around in the fractured language of the play, and he unearths a very multifaceted protagonist. This is far from a singularly purposeful Hamm, steely and fascistic but just inevitably tied to the dying world. However, what might have been Rylance's attempts to bring depth to the role unfortunately sometimes manifests instead only as breadth. Why might Hamm, for example, occasionally speak in a German accent, as a Cockney or an Upper Class English gent? While there was, on the night I saw it, only one instance of each of these experimental invocations, this was perhaps more than enough. At times such as these Rylance's Hamm can come across as an exercise in character study, in making a character as complex as possible, but where this might only mean as diverse as possible. Where Rylance does make this approach work to his advantage is when presenting Hamm as the self-conscious ham actor. Here Hamm's observing himself 'play' is well played, and such self-reflexive and performative moments become highlights.

A comparable exercise in intentional obstacles was the decision to give Hamm prosthetic legs. Rylance apparently played the entire play with his legs tucked up under him on the old reddish-brown leather chair (another impressive aspect to the set, the battered chair resembling the bruised and barely beating heart of the play), and two lifeless limbs fractionally distinct from his real legs dangled from the chair without touching the floor. This did provide an apt visualisation of the dead weight that is Hamm's speciality (that he cannot stand). But it was even more effective in imputing to Hamm an air of maddened infantile, as his legs swung about a little like an impatient child's. Given the proximity of Hamm's binned parents the prop nicely underscored Hamm's menace and impotence.

Along with the two leads Tom Hickey as Nagg also managed to contrive some comedic physicality to accompany his language, in his shuffling rapidly on his 'stumps' between facing front and to the side, depending on where his attention was focussed. Both he and Miriam Margolyes as Nell gave a convincing portrayal of the aged rambling romantics, playing the parents as so many do as inflected with a little Irish.

Complicite, and particularly McBurney, have gone to great lengths to stage this production, which was originally scheduled to have Richard Briers as Hamm and Adrian Scarborough as Clov. Both pulled out due to conflicting commitments. Though the two had never worked together McBurney approached Rylance backstage at a performance of *Jerusalem* to ask if he might play Hamm. Rylance, although he had never previously performed Beckett (or by that point read much other than *Murphy* and *Waiting for Godot* many years earlier), knew of and admired Complicite, and agreed to collaborate. But unfortunately this same spirit of mutual admiration that managed to rescue the production hovers around it rather like the ominous smoke at the performance's start. There is obvious respect between the two, but a tangible gulf as well that looks at times like one of understanding. It becomes clear these are two very different creatures. Similarly to how Hamm's characterisation is occasionally forced through an ill-fitting accent or two, the pseudo-couple's interaction is at times subject to a mutual exploration which does not seem entirely intrinsic to the play. However, this situation can also bring rewards. For example, when the two argue in a more explicitly hierarchical context their deliveries appear more precisely poised, their purpose more tightly formulated as they size themselves and each other up.

The performance was followed by a question and answer session with the cast, one of two held during the seventy performances in the run. Questions focused on how the rest of the cast felt working with a multi-tasking director and actor, variations between *Endgame* and *Fin de partie*, and the play's physical demands. One question that raised some debate involved how the play might have 'accrued different meanings' since its first performance more than fifty years earlier, when that bare stage was such a shock. In contrast to how some awkward questions put to Ian McKellan and Patrick Stewart on BBC2's *Culture Show* about how *Waiting for Godot* might speak to the credit crunch were batted away with references to 'universality', Rylance described the 'corpsed' world outside the room as one in which climate change had wreaked havoc. Keen to instil a return to 'fundamental sounds', Hickey tried to balance this by retelling the story (found in Deidre Bair's biography) according to which Beckett reportedly said Hamm and Clov were 'himself and Suzanne', emphasising the surprising interpretative possibilities of the play and un-resolvability of such issues.

If the mutual appreciation between McBurney and Rylance restrained this production's potential to be a truly great one, proscribing it boundaries it would have been more impressive to see broken down, they still staged a thoughtful and respectful performance. It is to be hoped that the company and Rylance, together or apart, try to take on Beckett once again.

David Tucker
DOI: 10.3366/E0309520710000695

INTERVIEW

Julie Campbell interviews Simon McBurney, director and actor (Clov) in *Endgame*, Duchess Theatre, London (October–December 2009).

JC: **How would you distinguish between the two roles of director and actor?**

SM: When you are an actor, you are totally focused on that job, you're not focused on the job as a director, and that directing part of you sort of happens at a different moment.

In relation to Samuel Beckett's work, I began as an actor and any actor who works in the theatre will inevitably at some point in their career pass by Beckett. I don't mean to say that everyone will do Beckett, or want to do Beckett, but they will have an encounter with Beckett, because it's extraordinary material and it challenges you. It also excites and stimulates and arouses you as an actor. There is a sensuality and a music to the language, which is extraordinarily enticing. And when I say a sensuality or musicality those are poor words because they tend towards a cliché of the imagined: you know with the sensual we tend to think of touch, but by sensual I mean there's a real feeling in the mouth and that is given, not only by the words themselves, but also by the rhythm and the percussion of them and the speed of exchange and by the silences they create. I think the fact of it is that language in Beckett is a protagonist; it's a character in itself. The language is what the audience are trying to make sense of – and they're teased by it, and amused by it – but the language is a character in its own right. So when you're performing, you have to do quite a complicated job because the language will have its own life. So you've got to bring somebody to the table eventually. So I'm very touched that you liked my portrayal of Clov, because I listened to the language and I spoke it, and we obeyed the pauses *absolutely*. I was insistent that everybody should feel the rhythm that Beckett creates on the page as a starting point, and not decide what we should do until that was really within our bodies. From that sensation within your body you can begin to let go and allow your own imagination to travel and somebody begins to arrive and then as that person arrives as an actor, as a character, so gradually you unfold and almost like a plant from the seed, the seed being the words and the rhythms and the accuracy of what I would call 'Beckett's DNA', from that can grow a character, which is almost like a plant. But it comes slowly. If you apply somebody too quickly to the material, it all starts to disintegrate. You have to go from the very, very inside and then something happens. Perhaps that is why sometimes vaudevillians like Max Wall can have an affinity with Beckett: they bring something of themselves from over a lifetime of doing a similar kind of act, and over a lifetime something arrives and in a way they can become a vessel for the words of Beckett and the words of Beckett can travel through them, rather than an actor who might apply too much interpretation, which is a different kind of skill really.

JC: **What have you discovered, directing and acting in *Endgame*?**

SM: I think that what I have discovered is something about the nature of his use of language. Language is the essence of man. The language of each character, the language of *Endgame*, is a kind of extraordinary mask, and when you begin to play the play you almost put the language on like a costume. It's not like the words, which are just simply spoken, the words are more additive than that. They are almost like the plot. And the words almost grab the speakers and imprison them, like fish in a net. So that they can't get away and all the way through they're looking for words – 'Have you anything else to say to me?' And the only words that come to Nagg are – 'Would you like your biscuit?' He's trapped by his own words. Hamm makes Clov look for a word to describe the outside world – corpsed. Does that mean there are thousands of bodies out there? Or just that it's dead. It's not clear but he finds a word.

JC: How about the way it's changed during the run?

SM: It's very simple. You begin by exploring an understanding. The structure and the framework of the words and the play, and you try to really adhere to what is being asked for. Then, gradually life comes into it and you begin to try to bring it alive in the way that you want to bring it alive. But it's a little bit like coming into an empty house and you want to bring that house, which already exists, alive in a way. So first of all you don't put anything in it. Then you might start painting the walls or you might do the opposite, you might start stripping them away to reveal what's actually there, take away all the things that you would normally decorate with and reveal the beauty of the bare brick work or the wooden stairs, or the beams, and actually reveal the quality of that building. But there comes a moment when you need a kitchen. You need to cook and you need to live in it – you can't just admire it. So gradually, slowly, sensitively you try to put things in there, which feel right. And you put something in and think 'that's not right, I'll take that out and put that in.' But it's a slow process. So how it's changed from when you last saw it, is basically that it's fuller. It's more full of detail: there are pictures on the walls. There is a familiarity with it. The bodies know where they're going. I know the objects. We constantly try to open ourselves to the play anew every night. We talk about it, we change things, we put in a new feeling here, a new emphasis there. Now it's really detailed and I think it's fuller and more surprising and funnier and sadder. You've got to live in this house, it's got to become yours. The challenge again is to make the words our own with all their force and pathos, identifying with that force and pathos. It's no use living in a house and thinking 'oh this is really beautiful'. It's got to somehow be yours. You've got to embody it, and really be it. And that takes time. And I think time is the one thing you really need when working with Beckett. You have to have a familiarity with it and also you have to have a tremendous openness to it.

DOI: 10.3366/E0309520710000701

NOTES ON CONTRIBUTORS

Mary Bryden is Professor of French Studies at the University of Reading. Her monographs include *Women in the Prose and Drama of Samuel Beckett: Her Own Other* and *Samuel Beckett and the Idea of God*, and she has recently co-edited (with Margaret Topping) the collection of essays entitled *Beckett's Proust/Deleuze's Proust* (Palgrave, 2009). She is currently editing *The Beckett Bestiary*, a collection of essays on Beckett and Animality.

Julie Campbell is Lecturer in Literature and Drama at the University of Southampton, UK. She has published widely, in books and scholarly journals, on Beckett's fiction and drama. Her essay on Beckett and Paul Auster was published in *Beckett at 100: Revolving It All* (Oxford UP, 2008), and her chapter '"A Voice Comes to One in the Dark: Imagine": Radio, the Listener and the Dark Comedy of All That Fall' was published in *Beckett and Death* (Continuum, 2009).

Gaby Hartel is a cultural historian and a fellow at the Zentrum für Literatur- und Kulturforschung, Berlin. She produces fiction and documentary programmes for German cultural radio, curates art exhibitions and is guest lecturer at the Royal Art Academy, Oslo and various German Universities. Her interest lies in the cross-over between media and literature and she co-curated the

Journal of Beckett Studies 19.2 (2010): 306–309
Edinburgh University Press
DOI: 10.3366/E0309520710000713
© The editors, *Journal of Beckett Studies*
www.eupjournals.com/jobs

show *Samuel Beckett/Bruce Nauman* at the Kunsthalle Wien in 2000. She has written widely on radio art, and her publications include her dissertation on Samuel Beckett as a visual artist, a monograph on Samuel Beckett, and essays on media artists, on silliness and walking as artistic strategies. Together with Michael Glasmeier, Gaby is currently editing a book on Beckett's film and television work. With Uta Kornmeier she recently established an interdisciplinary research project on the psychoaesthetics of city sounds at the Zentrum für Literatur- und Kulturforschung, Berlin.

Thomas Hunkeler is Professor of French and Comparative Literature at the University of Fribourg (Switzerland). He is the author of *Echos de l'ego dans l'œuvre de Samuel Beckett* (Harmattan, 1997) and *Le vif du sens. Corps et poésie selon Maurice Scève* (Droz, 2003) and the editor of *Le Drame du regard. Théâtralité de l'œuvre d'art* (Peter Lang, 2002) and *Place au public. Les spectateurs du théâtre contemporain* (MetisPresses, 2008).

Thomas Irmer was editor-in-chief of the monthly journal *Theater der Zeit* from 1998 to 2003 and teaches American drama and theatre at Freie Universität Berlin, Germany. He has published numerous articles on Beckett in Germany and also contributed to *The International Reception of Samuel Beckett*, ed. by Mark Nixon and Matthew Feldman (Continuum, 2009). Forthcoming is a book of conversations with the theoretician Andrzej Wirth about his life and work in Poland, the United States and Germany.

Tine Koch is writing her PhD thesis at the University of Hamburg under the supervision of Dr. Barbara Müller-Wesemann and Prof. Dr. Jörg Schönert. Her thesis provides a comparative study of Samuel Beckett's and Thomas Bernhard's dramatic variations of the *'theatrum-mundi'*-topos, and as a part of this she explores the influence of German Romanticism in Beckett's specific use of the 'play' theme.

Charles Krance has published a number of articles and essays on Beckett (in English and French), and is founding editor of the Samuel Beckett's Bilingual Works series of genetic editions, which are currently taking on a significantly innovative electronic dimension, under the skilful guidance of Dirk Van Hulle and Mark Nixon.

Mark Nixon is Lecturer in English at the University of Reading, where he is also the Director of the Beckett International Foundation. He is an editor of *Samuel Beckett Today / Aujourd'hui*, review editor of the *Journal of Beckett Studies*, and the Co-Director of the Beckett Digital Manuscript Project. He has recently prepared, for Faber & Faber, an edition of Beckett's *Texts for Nothing and Other Short Prose 1950–1976* (2010). He is currently editing *Publishing Samuel Beckett* (British Library, 2010) and working on *Samuel Beckett's Library* (Cambridge UP, 2011) with Dirk Van Hulle. His monograph *Samuel Beckett's 'German Diaries'* will be published by Continuum in 2011, and his critical edition of Beckett's unpublished short story 'Echo's Bones' is appearing with Faber in 2011.

John Pilling is Emeritus Professor of English and European Literature at the University of Reading, where he was Director of the Beckett International Foundation, which he now serves in an advisory capacity. He is a former Editor of the *Journal of Beckett Studies*, on whose Advisory Board he still serves. He is also a member of the Advisory Board for *Samuel Beckett Today/Aujourd'hui*, which has published several of his essays. His books include: *In A Strait Of Two Wills: Beckett's More Pricks Than Kicks* (forthcoming); *A Samuel Beckett Chronology* (2006); *A Companion to 'Dream of Fair to Middling Women'* (2004); *Beckett Before Godot* (1997); *Frescoes of the Skull: the later prose and drama of Samuel Beckett* (1979; with James Knowlson); and *Samuel Beckett* (1976). He has contributed more than thirty essays to journals, symposia and collections of various kinds, and is currently researching Beckett's life and work in the 1930s.

David Tucker is an Associate Tutor at the University of Sussex. He has published on Beckett in *Samuel Beckett Today/Aujourd'hui* and contributed to the collections *Publishing Samuel Beckett*, *Dictionnaire Samuel Beckett* and *The Tragic Comedy of Samuel Beckett*. He is the editor of *British Social Realism Since 1940* (forthcoming 2011).

Dirk Van Hulle is associate professor of English literature at the University of Antwerp, where he works at the Centre for Manuscript Genetics. He is president of the European Society for Textual Scholarship, board member of the Beckett Society, and co-director of the Beckett Digital Manuscript Project. He has recently prepared an edition of Beckett's *Company, Ill Seen Ill Said, Worstward Ho, Stirrings Still* (Faber & Faber, 2009). His research and publications focus on the writing methods of twentieth-century authors and include the monographs *Textual Awareness* (2004) and *Manuscript Genetics: Joyce's Know-How, Beckett's Nohow* (2008). He is an editor of the *Journal of Beckett Studies* and *Samuel Beckett Today / Aujourd'hui*, and is currently working on *Samuel Beckett's Library* (Cambridge UP, 2011) with Mark Nixon.

Shane Weller is Reader in Comparative Literature and Co-Director of the Centre for Modern European Literature at the University of Kent. His publications include *A Taste for the Negative: Beckett and Nihilism* (2005), *Beckett, Literature, and the Ethics of Alterity* (2006), and *Literature, Philosophy, Nihilism: The Uncanniest of Guests* (2008). He is also the editor of *Molloy* in the Faber & Faber edition of Beckett's works.

Now available from

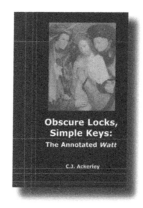

EU Authorised Representative:

Easy Access System Europe Mustamäe tee 50, 10621 Tallinn, Estonia

gpsr.requests@easproject.com

Printed and bound by CPI Group (UK) Ltd, Croydon, CR0 4YY

09/06/2025

01897302-0001